YOUTH!
THE 26%
SOLUTION

BY

WENDY SCHAETZEL LESKO

ACTIVISM 2000 PROJECT

&

EMANUEL TSOUROUNIS, II

YOUTH! THE 26% SOLUTION
Printed in the United States of America.
Published by the ACTIVISM 2000 PROJECT,
Information U.S.A., Inc.
P.O. Box E, Kensington, MD 20895

Graphic design by randio
          847-763-1303
          www.randio.com

Cover illustration by Nicholas E. Galifianakis

ISBN #1-878346-47-4
First Edition, 1998

For bulk rates or custom editions, contact:
ACTIVISM 2000 PROJECT
Toll-Free: 1-800-543-7693

To all the youth who dare to care

ACKNOWLEDGEMENTS

We thank all the young activists whose true stories fill and enrich **YOUTH! THE 26% SOLUTION.** Their contributions are a source of great inspiration to us and provide further proof that young people can be uniquely influential, especially with people in positions of power.

A big hand also goes out to those who found the time in between exams, college applications, and the busy winter holiday to review an early draft of this action guide. Each of these reviewers gave such honest feedback and so many superb suggestions that we revised nearly every page. Our sincere appreciation to all of them:

> **Erica Bellamy,** editor of "Children's Express," Indianapolis, Indiana, and student at Park Tutor School
>
> **Annie Brody,** Vice President of National Programs, Earth Force, Alexandria, Virginia
>
> **Carol Burgoa,** Prevention Coordinator, Contra Costa County Office of Education, Pleasant Hills, California
>
> **Marqueece L. Dawson,** Director of Youth Programs, Community Coalition, Los Angeles, California
>
> **Jared Feldman,** student at Mount View Middle School, Marriottsville, Maryland
>
> **Kathryn W. Johnson,** Director of Evaluation, Alternatives, Inc., Hampton, Virginia
>
> **Lucy Merritt,** Co-President of Kirkwood Youth Service and student at Kirkwood High School, St. Louis, Missouri
>
> **Maxine Amber Norcross,** middle school student at Sidwell Friends School, Washington, D.C.
>
> **Ben Smilowitz,** Co-Founder of the International Student Activism Alliance and student at Hall High School, West Hartford, Connecticut
>
> **Trang Vu,** student at McMain Magnet Secondary School, New Orleans, Louisiana

Please consider sending us news of what you have done or are doing. With your permission, our national clearinghouse would like to pass along news of your campaign to others who are trying to solve similar problems in their corner of the world. As an added incentive, if you submit a true story that is included in a future edition of **YOUTH! THE 26% SOLUTION** or any other ACTIVISM 2000 PROJECT book, you will receive as many free copies of that publication as you want.

TABLE OF CONTENTS

Showcase of Youth Productions

I N T R O D U C T I O N

The 26% Solution = The YOUTH Solution

According to the U.S. Census Bureau, 68 million people in the United States are under the age of 18. That's **26%** of the population who participate in **school and community activities**, **26%** who spend more than **$150 billion a year**, and **26%** who **care about the world** in which they live. However, that's also **26%** of the population who **cannot vote** and **26%** who are supposed to be **seen and not heard**, making for a resounding **100% of the future** who have not been encouraged to **exercise leadership today**.

Shouldn't young people—who are citizens, students, and consumers— have a **voice** in issues that directly concern them?

Shouldn't this 26% of the population be able to participate in the **decision-making** process?

Shouldn't the quarter of the population with firsthand knowledge of the many problems facing our schools, communities, and society be involved in the **search for solutions** — RIGHT NOW?

YOU NO LONGER HAVE TO BE SHUT OUT.

Youth want to participate and more adults recognize that the long tradition of **making decisions for youth without youth has failed.** Community and business leaders as well as government organizations realize their efforts to deal with concerns such as **pollution, substance abuse, drunk driving, failing schools,** and **violence** are much more effective when young people have contributed their ideas and are involved in solving these problems. You can make a difference, whether you take the initiative as a single individual, as a member of a youth or school organization, or as part of an alliance with other students and adults.

Getting decision-makers to take you seriously is not as difficult as you might expect.

It's knowing enough about the system and how it works so you can influence it. **YOUTH! THE 26% SOLUTION** suggests different ways to pinpoint the problem, design solutions, create a plan, and accomplish your goals. Inspiring stories drawn from the experiences of hundreds of young activists who have turned their passion into action are included along with creative strategies that show how to use your age to your advantage. Hundreds of organizations, such as national advocacy groups and news media outlets, are also listed to serve as resources for your campaign. You can either read this book from beginning to end or dive right into the sections that deal with what you are trying to accomplish at the moment. Then, jot down your thoughts in "Download Your Brain" in Chapter 5, or in the margins — wherever you want.

So, enjoy and remember: **THE 26% SOLUTION** is a "**YOU**"th solution. Si se puede...Yes, it can be done!

Wendy Schaetzel Lesko

Emanuel Tsourounis, II

NO INVITATION REQUIRED!

Right now in your community, numerous efforts are underway to improve the school system, combat crime, protect the environment, and design new approaches to deal with old problems. One initiative may be led by a few people in the neighborhood, another by community and business leaders in town. Perhaps a special task force or commission has been established by your mayor or school superintendent to make recommendations to address a specific problem. Despite the huge push by adults, few will consider the merit of involving youth or getting their input, even when the problems and decisions directly affect them. It's not that they don't want to include you, they haven't thought to.

No matter. **Don't wait for an invitation!** Some problems are too important to leave to adults alone to solve. If what's happening affects you, you can and should be involved. The opportunity exists for you to join forces with adults or to start your own youth-driven campaign. Our democracy is not a spectator sport. It depends on ordinary people who are willing to get involved and stick their necks out. Besides, you have the power to make a change.

Never underestimate the value of the contribution you can make.

Being young, you have an advantage! You have the inside "scoop" on your generation. You know what concerns youth, which programs work well and which don't, and how policies and services impact people in your age group. Consider yourself an expert! Also, your frank and direct approach will win respect. Genuine concern is rarely questioned, unlike lobbyists and other professionals who are paid to represent others.

In addition, being young means you do not need to be conventional and play by all of the adult rules. You can challenge traditional attitudes and thinking, which tend to restrict and limit adults. **Be innovative and creative.** Your solutions and actions can reflect your idealism or pragmatism and be imaginative or practical — whatever the situation calls for. To adults, your perspective will be something new and different and your ideas fresh.

Don't worry if, at first, adults don't seem to take you seriously. Many times, parents and teachers may warn you against doing something because they do not wish to see you fail. You may wonder, "Why am I doing this? It will never work." Decision-makers may not listen because they don't think you have enough experience to know what you are talking about. But you do and **you CAN make a difference**. Negative stereotypes about youth run deep, but **just because you are a minor does not mean you cannot play a major role.** Be persistent and patient. Your effort will teach adults that youth can do it and, in the process, you also may achieve something positive for your school, community, the environment, society, and maybe even the world! To care and be dedicated are all you need. You don't need any special skills or training. There are no invitations, either!

C H A P T E R I
Preparing to Act Up

Aside from death and taxes, nothing is more certain than change. Everything changes: people, society, the environment, our world. What isn't so certain, however, is the role you will play in creating or supporting change, or resisting it. Change won't happen spontaneously. Even limited projects, attempts at small improvements, or major reforms occur because of the concerted efforts of people — not only those in positions of authority, but those sitting at home or at a conference reading this book. People like you!

As activists, you will be interested in **promoting positive change,** the kind of change that results in **g r o w t h , d e v e l o p m e n t , a n d r e n e w a l** , that helps rather than hurts, and is best for everyone, not just a select few. Activists want to change attitudes and actions, beliefs and behaviors, at a personal, local, and global level. That means they deal with a number of important issues, such as injustice and inequality, and promote awareness of the problems, propose solutions, and, in some instances, lobby for new or improved laws.

Action is the key. Nothing happens by wishing, hoping, thinking or dreaming. **Being a dreamer and a doer is the winning combination.** Chances are, you can name a few things you would like to see changed (or not changed) around you. Once an idea hits, act! There is no single step-by-step formula on how best to proceed, but this chapter suggests some ways for you to get started.

There are all sorts of reasons and motivations to get involved. It might be the excitement of a promising idea or your appreciation for the environment. Being upset or angry may cause people to speak up for their rights or the rights of others. Other times, people are propelled to action by dissatisfaction with an existing program or service. You may want to take a stand on proposals being debated in your state legislature to restrict learner's permits and revoke driver's licenses. A story on TV or an article in the newspaper can awaken a concern, an interest, or a sense of responsibility.

DIFFERENT MOTIVATIONS

In 1995, TWELVE-YEAR-OLD Craig Kielburger of Toronto read about the death of Iqbal Masih, a boy his age in Pakistan who had spent six years chained to a rug loom. Masih had escaped these slave-like conditions and then fought to change this horrifying practice, even speaking before the General Assembly of the United Nations, but was later assassinated. This tragedy caused Kielburger to take action. The young Canadian started an international organization called "Free The Children" which continues to mount a worldwide campaign against child labor.

26% at work

A FRESHMAN from Hempstead High School in Dubuque, Iowa, collected 650 student and staff signatures demanding doors be placed on the individual stalls in the boys' bathrooms. The school board agreed. New stalls with doors will be installed when the restrooms are remodeled so that they meet requirements of the Americans with Disabilities Act.

In Leesburg, Virginia, several 14 AND 15-YEAR-OLDS were angry that in-line skaters and skateboarders were banned from using sidewalks, parking lots and just about every other stretch of pavement. The boys decided to voice their complaints to their town council and also asked for some place to skate. The decision-makers listened. Three of the teenagers were selected to serve on a parks committee and worked with architects and others to design a skating facility.

PUZZLING PROBLEMS AND SHAPING SOLUTIONS

There's no shortage of issues...

Hunger
Car crashes Police
Jails Pollution Gun violence
Curfews Cloning Anorexia
nervosa Landfills Gangs Toxic waste
Homophobia   Internet
Deforestation   Runaways
Truancy   Graffiti
Poverty   Drugs
Pregnancy   Rehab Litter
                    Abortion
                    Obesity
                  TV ratings
                  Pesticides
                  Puppy mills
                Censorship
                Date rape
                Detention
                Racism
                Inhalants
                Dropouts
              Dress code
              Depression
              Hate crime
              Divorce
              Addiction
          Libraries Child abuse AIDS Stress
          Immigration   Endangered species
          Adoption   Affirmative   Action

Global
warming
Malnutrition
Sweatshops
Job training
Welfare
CO$_2$ Ozone
Bulimia
Shoplifting
Air   quality
Teacher   evaluations Peer
counseling School-based health
clinics Conflict resolution Chewing
tobacco Bilingual   education
Secondhand smoke   Global population
United Nations   Metal detectors
Bicycle lanes   Multiculturalism
Safe havens   Homelessness
College tuition   Mass transit
School prayer   Driver's Ed
School vouchers   Taxes Bullies
Binge drinking   Juvenile justice
Loitering in malls   Domestic violence
Death   penalty   Health insurance
Substance abuse Corporal punishment
Locker searchers   Sexual harassment
School bathrooms Discrimination
Economic development Suicide
Graduation requirements

You may have already pinpointed a key concern of yours and identified the problem. Jot it down. (Go to "Download Your Brain" at the end of the last chapter. It is meant for exactly this purpose). If you aren't sure yet what problem you want to work with, try making a list of issues that interest you. Choose broad categories and then dissect them into their parts, like a puzzle. Pick the ones that affect you or your community or that you feel strongly about and would like to dedicate your time and effort to.

If you are still stumped, try asking your friends and family. Do a little community exploring. Survey your neighbors and ask them what they would like to see happen, what needs they may have, and what things they are unhappy with. You could also see what other groups are trying to do. Contact the department of parks and recreation, the county health agency, or your mayor's office. Who knows? You might be able to find a group with similar interests and concerns.

As you brainstorm, you'll probably see connections between all of the different issues and problems which may, at first, seem puzzling. Don't worry. Many issues and problems are closely linked, if not related. Some may even be the causes or consequences of others. Just keep thinking, making notes of your initial thoughts and perhaps a few key words. They are likely to spur ideas, and may be modified later as you dig deeper into the problem. If they are bold and compelling, your original words and descriptions can be useful in a letter, speech, recruitment flyer, or in your evaluation months from now.

> **"A problem is a chance for you to do your best."**
> — Duke Ellington

Once you have decided on the one problem you want to address, it's time to shape a solution. Before you do, think about the time, money, and effort you will need to commit. Are you being realistic? Imagine the possible consequences, both positive and negative. Assess the political "weather"— who will support this solution and who won't? Also, determine what kind of impact you want to have and on whom? When you are ready, consider your options:

 ### TREATING THE CAUSE, NOT THE SYMPTOMS:

If you want to get to the root of the problem, most likely it will mean addressing **related issues**. Concern about crime and violence might move you to **look beyond** metal detectors and handgun restrictions to working for better schools and more job opportunities. This initiative could take a long time to achieve, but proposing one experimental pilot project in your neighborhood could produce results quickly.

LOOKING AT THE PROBLEM, PIECE-BY-PIECE:
You can concentrate on **one aspect** of the problem to avoid getting bogged down. When you have accomplished what you wanted, you can move on to another aspect of the problem and propose another solution. Often solutions that address one particular problem or part of a problem can be the **first of many** steps, leading to more massive change. Certainly, Rosa Park's refusal to sit in the back of the bus in Montgomery, Alabama, proved to be a key event in the civil rights movement of the 1960's.

 PREVENTION VS. INTERVENTION:
Another way to break down a problem is to consider whether you are most concerned about **stopping** it from happening or **dealing** with the problem once it has occurred. **Multiple solutions are almost always necessary:** students concerned with AIDS might decide to try to change the school district's overall health education curriculum, while others might decide to concentrate their efforts on providing greater access to HIV testing and teen counseling.

By knowing your limitations and clarifying your goals, you will have a better sense of how you can handle the problem and what could work best.

After a little while, you'll have brainstormed a number of ideas. Try to focus on one or two. Run them by a few of your friends, a trusted teacher, or a parent. Be careful whom you talk to about your initial plan or possible solution — not because someone might steal your idea, but because **new concepts are fragile. Avoid naysayers.** Gauge people's interest. Listen and absorb constructive comments. But, if the responses are not very enthusiastic, don't let that stop you from taking action. A racial incident, a toxic landfill, and many other problems are overlooked and ignored until someone succeeds at getting them on the public radar screen. **THAT SOMEONE CAN BE YOU.**

Students at WEST BRANCH MIDDLE SCHOOL in Iowa save the school nearly $250 a month on electricity by using energy-saving T8 light bulbs. However, their effort to cut electrical usage in all schools was initially met with resistance by the local school board. The student proposal called for a low-interest loan to pay for the bulbs and to convert the outlets. After four months of persistent lobbying by students, the cautious school board members approved the plan.

Common Sense Solutions

26% at work

Remember the first TOYS-FOR-GUNS EXCHANGE? This gun amnesty program in New York City has been replicated in Los Angeles, Washington, D.C., and a number of other cities. This initiative was the brainchild of A 14-YEAR-OLD BOY whose father listened and, together, they mobilized their community to act.

EIGHTH GRADERS in Walnut, California, researched drought-resistant landscaping as a way to conserve water. They sent handwritten notes to hundreds of newspapers, water districts, and influential individuals and then traveled to the State Capitol. These conservationists convinced lawmakers to pass a bill requiring all state government buildings to use only water-saving plants.

ADDRESSING THE ISSUE OF TRUANCY

Trang Vu, along with other high school students participating in the New Orleans Police Department Pre-Cadet Program, examined why so many students skip class and drop out of school. In addressing the issue, they looked at the causes and consequences of student truancy and focused on solutions that would prevent or provide intervention. Their findings, along with this chart, received serious consideration from the Police Chief and other important city officials.

CAUSES:	CONSEQUENCES:
- Lack of enthusiasm - School environment - Personal problems - Lack of parental involvement	- Truants turn bad - Delinquency - Violence - Unemployment/dropout rate rises - Uneducated work force

PREVENTION:	INTERVENTION:
- Teachers' methods/educational background - Parental/community involvement - Social workers to visit family/home - Provide bulletin/newsletter	- Renovation of schools - Penalize students, vendors, teachers and security guards that aid/serve truants - Better security - Counseling/parent-teacher conferences - Community service or jail time

THE 26% SOLUTION

26 IDEAS FOR CHANGE INITIATED BY 26% OF THE POPULATION

The possibilities are endless, but here are a few suggestions (of course, only you know best what is needed where you live).

Explore with city planners the need for additional youth recreational services: after-school programs, a teen community center, midnight basketball leagues, etc.

■ ■ ■ ■

Meet with local officials about making roads safer for pedestrians and bicyclists: installing stop signs, speed bumps, traffic lights, sidewalks, bike lanes and trails.

■ ■ ■ ■

Help keep your public library open longer hours by writing letters of support to your city or county council members and the news media.

■ ■ ■ ■

Clean up streams and waterways: measure pollutants and share this data with environmental regulators, community groups, area developers, and farmers.

■ ■ ■ ■

Work to improve your school (Internet access, course offerings, cleaner bathrooms, better cafeteria food, etc.) by starting your own organization or working with student clubs, the PTA, school administrators, and the board of education.

■ ■ ■ ■

Lobby to get a student member with full voting rights on both your local school board and the state board of education.

■ ■ ■ ■

Help improve counseling services at school and in the community by starting a 24-hour teen hotline, a school-based health center, or a stress management program.

■ ■ ■ ■

Produce a pamphlet, video, or public service announcement about abstinence, sexually transmitted diseases, or other health issues that can add to what is taught in school.

■ ■ ■ ■

YOUTH!

Create and perform a theatrical skit or play about sexual harassment, homophobia, or gender stereotypes for community groups and political leaders.

■ ■ ■ ■

Survey your neighborhood for the number of liquor stores, beer outlets, alcohol ads, and billboards; share your findings with the zoning commission and news media.

■ ■ ■ ■

Contact your local police precinct or the Police Chief to discuss community policing and other programs intended to reduce truancy, drug abuse, graffiti, gangs, etc.

■ ■ ■ ■

Train to be a peer mediator at your school to help resolve conflicts and share your ideas on how to improve the school district's violence prevention policies and programs.

■ ■ ■ ■

Create a teen court in which youth judge and sentence their peers who have pled guilty to shoplifting and other non-violent offenses.

■ ■ ■ ■

Address racism and prejudice by forming a group that sponsors school or community events to stop discrimination and celebrate diversity.

■ ■ ■ ■

Launch a "Teens as Teachers" speakers' bureau on an issue you care about (eating disorders, child abuse prevention, rainforest preservation, etc.).

■ ■ ■ ■

Conduct a poll throughout the entire school district on specific education issues, such as whether to begin the high school day later rather than earlier, and publicize the results to the school board and county PTA.

■ ■ ■ ■

Speak to school, religious, and youth groups about freedom of speech and the effect of censorship of student newspapers, radio and TV programs, etc.

■ ■ ■ ■

Investigate how easy it is for minors to buy cigarettes or chewing tobacco at gas stations and stores; share your findings with the city or county council.

■ ■ ■ ■

Testify on proposed local and state legislation that affect youth (a nighttime curfew or a proposal to suspend or revoke a driver's license, etc.).

■ ■ ■ ■

Hold a candidates' forum where youth ask questions of those running for school board, city hall, etc., followed by an election. Release the results of this youth vote to the press.

■ ■ ■ ■

Form a local chapter of the International Student Activism Alliance, SADD, Student Coalition Against Tobacco or another youth-run organization. Plan events and speak up about issues affecting young people.

■ ■ ■ ■

Lobby the shopping mall management to consider changing certain policies—for instance, mall security guards' treatment of teenage patrons—or convince them of the need for job training opportunities for students.

■ ■ ■ ■

Participate in the global campaign against child labor by boycotting products made in slave-like conditions and by supporting projects to create alternative sources of income for families.

■ ■ ■ ■

Seek to become a member of a community coalition, special task force, or citizen's committee such as the Mayor's Youth Advisory Council, Youth Commission, etc.

■ ■ ■ ■

Contact local foundations or businesses about starting a mini-grant program to improve community services, and have students who are trained in judging applications be involved in deciding what youth proposals should be funded.

■ ■ ■ ■

Host a city-wide youth summit to explore possible solutions to serious problems, such as teen suicide, gun violence, homelessness, unemployment, failing schools, etc., and invite the news media to attend.

YOUTH!

JOINING A TEAM OR BUILDING YOUR OWN

As you think more about what you'd like to do, you might consider getting some help, too. That will likely take you in a few different directions. For instance, you may hear of an organization or group that is concerned with the same problem that interests you. You can definitely try to join their team or form an alliance with them. Perhaps you will choose, instead, to form a team of your own. Joining a team or building your own can be a major decision, and there are plenty of advantages and disadvantages of each that you should investigate before you decide.

1

JOINING UP WITH AN ADULT-RUN ORGANIZATION:

Times are changing. More adults are growing comfortable with the idea of working with youth as partners. They realize the value of your input and want to channel your energy *and* benefit from your willingness to contribute. An increasing number of community-based agencies and organizations are including youth, even on their boards of directors. Some may even have a staff person whose main job is to recruit students to work with them.

To get involved, all you have to do is let a group know you're interested. A well-established organization can mean more resources, opportunities, and allies. Adults can often "open doors" because they have personal contacts with politicians and other community leaders. One potential drawback, however, is that adults may outnumber the students on board, and you may be expected to do what they want. An organization's goals and rules may limit the range of activities and actions you can pursue.

A FEW SUCCESSFUL YOUTH–ADULT PARTNERSHIPS:
The Regional Youth/Adult Substance Abuse Project based in Bridgeport, Connecticut; Earth Force's Youth Advisory Board; National Network for Youth; many local community partnerships such as Neighborhood Watch; local chapters of national organizations from the Urban League to the Humane Society view youth as equal partners.

MERGING WITH ANOTHER LIKE-MINDED GROUP:

2 Another option for you to explore is whether a club at your school or the student council/government is already involved with some of the same issues you are concerned about. If not, find out about the goals of some of the organizations in your community. By doing so, you'll probably discover several groups that are active and want to cooperate. Take the time to learn about the group and what it is trying to accomplish. See if its members are interested in what you are trying to do and want to work with you.

If the group already is well-known and has community support, it can provide a major headstart for your campaign. Also, there is strength in numbers. As a warning though, it can be a real challenge when joining with another organization to reach agreement on what should be done. You may disagree about what is needed to solve a problem or how best to approach a situation. Be on the lookout for other leaders who might have strong egos or who do not share the same goals or values.

A MUTUALLY BENEFICIAL ALLIANCE:

The International Student Activism Alliance (ISAA) with its concerns about censorship, curfews, and many other youth-related constitutional issues has ties with the Connecticut Civil Liberties Union. In return for their support, the ISAA gets some financial and technical support from the state affiliate of the American Civil Liberties Union.

FORMING AN INDEPENDENT YOUTH-LED GROUP: **3**

This option gives you the freedom to pursue your vision of how to make a difference without having a group of adults or a national organization calling the shots. Even though an independent student-run group may stand out because of its uniqueness, one disadvantage is that you will have to work harder in order to be taken seriously and win recognition. There's fun and also challenge in figuring out everything on your own — with the help of other concerned youth, of course.

YOUTH-RUN AND MANAGED ORGANIZATIONS:

National groups include Free The Children located in New York City, Kids For A Clean Environment (Kids F.A.C.E.) based in Tennessee, the Student Coalition Against Tobacco headquartered in West Virginia; examples of local groups are ERASE in New Jersey, whose members fight racism, and Helping Hands in Pinellas County, Florida, which provides assistance to teenagers with eating disorders.

YOUTH!

If you do decide to launch your own campaign rather than join forces with an existing organization or coalition, start recruiting now. Scout for other students at your school. Look for people who share your interest right in your own neighborhood, at the grocery store or theater, and at places of worship. Make sure to contact community youth groups such as the Boys and Girls Club. Go and speak at one of their meetings. By involving others, you can increase the brainpower and divide up what needs to be done. Working as a T.E.A.M.,**Together Everyone Achieves More!**

> **"Never doubt that a small group of thoughtful, committed citizens can change the world; indeed it's the only thing that ever has."**
> **— Margaret Mead**

Besides word-of-mouth recruitment, there are tons of other ways to attract friends and strangers from school and the community to get involved. Some strategies for getting the word out include:

- setting up a time and date for public meetings (choose a location that is safe, convenient, and large enough to accommodate a group that could grow in size)
- making a morning announcement over the P.A. system at school
- putting up flyers on bulletin boards at school, the supermarket, library, and elsewhere in your community
- posting a message on the school Web page
- sending out e-mail messages
- writing an article for the school newspaper
- sending the *same* article to other school newspapers
- submitting the *same* article to the neighborhood newsletter
- sending a short announcement to the weekly community newspaper
- asking the youth section of your daily newspaper to run a notice or article

making a pitch over the school TV news program

■ ■ ■

contacting the student government and other clubs at your school and in the school district

■ ■ ■

speaking with teachers, extracurricular advisors, and program coordinators

■ ■ ■

engaging groups like the PTA and perhaps student/parent community action groups

■ ■ ■

distributing information to youth directors, youth ministers, and other community group organizers

■ ■ ■

sending local radio stations a 10- or 20-second public service announcement about upcoming activities and meetings of your group

The more you publicize, the more other students and adults will take notice and want to get involved. Ideally, you will want to attract a lot of attention, but try to keep your team small and diverse. You will also want to keep things **manageable,** so watch out for things like:

① TEAM SIZE

It is easiest to work with a core group numbering between five and fifteen. Larger groups tend to be more difficult to handle—communication becomes a hassle, meetings are harder to plan because of conflicting schedules among members, and differences of opinions may be tougher to resolve. However, never turn away an enthusiast.

② TEAM DIVERSITY

Try to broaden your group to include people from various ethnic, social, and economic backgrounds. Try to recruit people who are directly impacted. For example, a substance abuse prevention project might seek input from a few students who have gone through drug treatment. The perspective each person brings to the campaign will be far greater this way and will strengthen the team.

YOUTH!

TEAM TALENTS 3

People who have different strengths and skills can help build and maintain momentum. Writers will be needed for penning letters and producing news releases. Artists can be illustrators, perhaps developing posters and flyers. People who like public speaking can take the spotlight and serve as spokespeople. Organizers should organize. Individuals may gravitate to assume responsibility for tasks that match their interest, but some shuffling may be necessary.

TEAM ORGANIZATION 4

Another decision that will need to be made is whether you want to function more as a team of co-chairs and committees or create a hierarchical structure with elected officers. Usually it is wise to have one person serve as the impartial facilitator who does not take sides during heated discussions and votes. You may also want to consider creating an adult advisory board as a way to further diversify your team but still have it be a youth-led initiative. Adults can still play an important role as allies, without stealing your thunder or controlling what happens.

Once you have your team, make it official. Create a name for your group or project. Make it easy to remember, but avoid abbreviations or acronyms that will not be understood. A brainstorming session by your core group is guaranteed to invent a catchy name. First collect some key words or phrases that describe what you hope to accomplish. Think about terms or expressions that will let others know that this is a youth-managed effort. Chances are a clever slogan may jump out at you from a list of words and phrases. (Some of the phrases may be

CAMPAIGN NAMES

LEAF IT TO US
The Utah student group that successfully lobbied Congress to pass a federal law providing matching funds to youth groups for planting trees.

▲

TEENS ON TARGET
Oakland, California youth who persuaded their city council to restrict the availability of handguns.

▲

PUFFLESS POTTIES
A campaign by Virginia students who were sick of smoky bathrooms at their high school.

▲

YOUTH ON BOARD
A national organization based in Boston that encourages non-profit organizations to include youth and students on their governing boards.

good to include when you develop a mission statement, news release, brochure, fundraising letter and other materials.)

Don't stop at a name. See if someone on the team likes to draw or can use some computer clip art to **create a logo** and **design letterhead**, perhaps even **business cards**. Include your group's name, a mailing address, phone number, an e-mail and Web address. Use this official stationery for mailings such as requests for endorsements or donations and letters to decision-makers. If your team has a clearly defined goal, go ahead and draft a mission statement or a wish list and put it on your letterhead (See suggestions on writing a mission statement in Chapter 2.) Otherwise, devote some time to research and planning before you set your objectives in stone.

MAKE IT OFFICIAL...
with a business card!

DOING THE DETECTIVE WORK

Information is golden, especially those hard-hitting facts and compelling statistics that will help you make your point and convince others that you are right. It is important that you remain open-minded and curious. Gather support from a number of different sources and even seek out contradictory evidence and conflicting numbers. By looking at the issue from all sides you can strengthen your argument and avoid being stumped by questions or being caught in embarrassing situations later on.

AS YOU RESEARCH, THINK ABOUT . . .

WHAT HAS BEEN TRIED before, and which ideas have **worked.**

AND WHICH HAVE NOT. Why was the idea successful or why wasn't it? If it wasn't, what were the **problems** and have they been addressed yet? Is there any new information or are there recent developments that support your position?

WHAT IS ALREADY HAPPENING. Is something being done to address the situation? Also, try to get a glimpse of the **bigger picture** by looking at what other communities, cities, and states are doing. Has someone come up with a unique or particularly **successful solution** to this problem? Can it be copied?

WHAT THE CONSEQUENCES MAY BE. Is what you are proposing beneficial? What will it **cost?** Whom will it **affect?** Do your projections match what others predict? If not, why are there differences?

WHAT OTHERS THINK. Do people in your community **agree** with you or do they disagree? Why? What do they suggest be done **differently?**

Also, do not limit your sources. Check out the listing of over 100 organizations and clearinghouses in the next chapter. Using old-fashioned research tools or high-tech strategies, you can get to know many experts and also collect loads of studies, reports, and other materials. In today's Information Age everyone has the same advantage—whether you live in a big city or far from a metropolitan hub.

TELEPHONING TIPS

The phone is so familiar, but calling strangers for information or to express yourself can be intimidating. **Try a two-step process**: first call to ask for the **name** and spelling of the person responsible for the issue you are concerned about. Then **call back** to speak to that individual. More than likely, your call will be transferred to that person because **you'll sound as though you know what you're doing.**

After introducing yourself, ask if the person has a few minutes to talk. If not, schedule a phone appointment by asking, "When would be a good time for you?" Keep a calendar to remind yourself.

Every telephone call will lead you from one person to another and, in turn, to another. Always ask, "Can you suggest others I should contact?" Then in later calls, do a bit of name dropping along the lines of "Hello, Ms. Vasquez. Eric King suggested I call you."

THE TELEPHONE remains one of the most effective research tools. Use it as though you are at a shopping mall. Just as getting the perfect gift requires browsing in many stores, you may need to call a lot of different people before you find exactly what you are looking for. So expect to make as many as a dozen calls. Check the phone book, particularly the blue pages that list government departments and agencies, and the yellow pages for businesses and associations.

THE INTERNET offers an infinite number of leads within seconds. Try a variety of search engines and experiment with different key words. Certainly the Web is a tremendous boom to gathering information about innovative programs and policies that exist around the country and even worldwide. Free access from your home, school, or public library makes this research tool amazing, but it's easy to get overwhelmed. Just remember you want to expand your knowledge base and don't lose sight of your mission.

SNAIL MAIL. A few postage stamps can generate pounds of information. Write to government and national organizations (refer to

OTHER TIPS...

☎ Avoid leaving messages if you cannot be reached during daytime hours. Instead, try calling again — repeatedly, if necessary.

☎ Before you make a call, jot down your key points. This way, you'll be sure to remember the important items that you want to discuss or ask.

☎ Identify yourself and mention the name of your group or organization. Even if you are working alone, give your project a name. This way your questions won't be dismissed as merely a school assignment.

☎ Keep a pencil and paper handy in case you want to make any notes.

Write down anything you think is important (contacts, references, etc.). Be sure to get the person's full name, address and phone number (in case your call has been transferred). It is always smart to keep a telephone log of everybody you speak with, including the receptionist. You never know—a few weeks or months later, you or someone else in your group might want to call back for more information.

☎ Be polite, but persistent, and you should have no problem expressing yourself over the phone. If it makes you feel better, practice beforehand. And, before you hang up, remember to thank whomever you are speaking to for their time and assistance.

the next chapter) to request statistics, studies, reports, referrals, and even videotapes. Ask if there are some exciting programs in other cities or states that seem effective in addressing particular problems. National groups can be helpful, suggesting individuals you should contact in your city or state.

YOUR OWN OBSERVATIONS AND SURVEYS can prove to be more persuasive than statistics and other research compiled by well-known organizations. Bolster your personal knowledge about a problem by obtaining information through interviews, surveys, questionnaires, focus groups, and polls. Even a small random sampling that does not meet standard research guidelines can be revealing. Don't discount your findings because this information can shed new light on a problem and increase support for specific solutions. Present your findings by writing a press release or formal summary statement along with charts, photographs or video footage.

TRACK DOWN EXPERTS. Contact various local agencies and organizations and ask to speak with the office of public affairs. Attend

Speedy Action on Student Survey

A youth-run county-wide campaign created an anonymous survey to collect confidential information. Fearing the Superintendent would not allow them to distribute their one-page questionnaire throughout the entire school district, the group found someone at every high school who got their principal's okay. Students filled out the questionnaire in English class, since every high school student takes this subject. Soon over 10,000 surveys were completed and the results were used to push for new school policies in Maryland.

Students Trash City's Waste Program

The Beachwood High School Ecology Club's investigation of the curbside recycling programs concluded that none of the 4,872 tons of residential trash in their Cleveland suburb was actually recycled. The findings were first disclosed in the school newspaper by Stephanie Bleyer, 16, who wrote, "Ladies and gentlemen of the city government, in the future when you sign an ambiguous contract [with Global Waste, Inc.] and advertise false city programs, give the whole true story or else student journalists like myself will." This evidence caused the mayor and others responsible to overhaul the city's solid waste reduction program.

26% at work

Research Gets Results

A student in Pojoaque, New Mexico, didn't want beer billboards near her school, so she contacted the state Office of Vital Statistics and other agencies to find out how many deaths in her county were alcohol-related, what percentage of those deaths involved underage drinkers, and how much the town was spending on drug education. Then she argued that the $11,000 spent for drug prevention was a waste and convinced the town to ban alcohol billboards near schools.

conferences and chat informally with speakers. Conduct interviews. Do a newspaper search and make notes of those community leaders and other authorities quoted in various stories. Call or write to them and the organizations mentioned in articles and also consider talking with the reporter to get additional background information. This information grapevine will definitely lead you to concerned citizens and people in decision-making positions who may become important supporters and potential allies.

PLAY "CONSTITUENT" if you are trying to change an existing law or policy or to get a new one passed. Even if your eighteenth birthday still is a few years away, in the minds of most elected officials you will be a voting constituent soon enough. Refer to the blue pages of your phone book, check with the public library, or call the League of Women Voters to find out the names and phone numbers of your city council members, school board members, state legislators, or U.S. representatives and senators. These elected officials have staff who are

first annual
youth health conference
in louisiana

AMBASSADOR SURVEY

This survey is for the sole purpose of gathering statistics. Because we may be using your answers as "real data" in the solution sessions, we ask that you be completely honest. We ask that you don't put your name anywhere on the survey. Thank you.

How old are you? _____

What city do you live in?_____

Do you attend public, private, or parochial school? _____

Do you feel that education in Louisiana is up to par? _____

ANONYMOUS SAMPLE QUESTIONNAIRE

QUESTIONS		
Do you know a teenager who is overweight?		
Do you know a teenager who is anorexic/bulimic?		
Are you overweight?		
Are you anorexic/bulimic?		
Have you ever cut class or skipped school?		
Do you personally know a teenager (age 13-19) who has died violently?		
Have you ever smoked a cigarette?		
Have you ever experimented with a drug?		
Have you ever seen a school social worker or psychiatrist?		
Have you ever contemplated suicide?		
Have you ever attempted suicide?		
Do you know someone who has?		

Where did you learn what you know about sex? (circle primary source)
a.) parent(s)   b.) peers   c.) school   d.) television   e.) other _____

What does the sex-education curriculum at your school include?
a) abstinence only   b) comprehensive

Do you know of at least two places where you can go to get information, testing and
       treatment for STDs, or counseling for/about sex, STDs and pregnancy? _____

*Thank you for your time and honesty! See you in the starter sessions. Enjoy the
conference from the Teen Sexuality Issue Committee (Johnica, Daniella, and Eric).*

easy to reach and can help with your research questions. For school issues, call the public school system's central office, and you will get referred to the office responsible for specific policies, such as school uniforms or teacher evaluations. Every town hall, county courthouse, and state capitol has a central information hub, sometimes called the legislative reference office. Many state legislatures operate toll-free numbers and also are accessible via the Internet. In a couple of minutes, they can search their databases and tell you anything you ever wanted to know about a particular bill (its author, who voted for or against it, what issues were presented at committee hearings and during floor debate, etc.). Then you can follow-up by contacting the individual elected officials and their staff.

Expect to get the run-around. It has nothing to do with your age... remember it takes an average of seven calls to reach the right person.

Your detective work will be ongoing. So continue to read the newspapers and watch the news, and stay in touch with your network of contacts. They can keep you informed of developments. The more you understand the issue, the better you will be able to communicate the findings of your research to others, especially decision-makers (you'll feel more confident, too). Your research will also likely prompt you to develop your solution further and move you closer to identifying who has the power to decide and who can help you in the process. (Identifying your audience and strategies for presenting your research are discussed in the next two chapters.)

C H A P T E R 2
From Dreaming to Doing

Once you've figured out **what** you want to do, you have to decide **how** you're going to do it! **Hard work and dedication at this stage will pay off later.** Decide who has the power to make a change, what your short and long term goals are, and determine how they'll get done and by whom. Also, don't hesitate to ask for help along the way— whether it is in the form of financial support or technical assistance that can be offered by adult allies or many of the national organizations listed at the end of this chapter. Good luck!

WHO'S GOT THE POWER?

Your campaign may put you on center stage, or at least in view of some important people who have decision-making power. You will be trying to convince them of the merits of your initiative or motivate them to help out, perhaps as a primary sponsor of your proposal. It's essential that you and your team **target** the right individuals who are responsible for calling the shots.

Whom you go to will have a lot to do with what you are trying to accomplish. For example, you wouldn't go to the President of the United States in order to change your school's discipline policy or dress code. You'd talk to your principal or members of the board of education. Or, if you wanted to persuade a national magazine not to advertise certain products or ask a company to stop testing its products on animals, you might direct your message to corporate headquarters and to stockholders. Sometimes, your initiative will bring you to the doorsteps of a number of VIPs, like the Chamber of Commerce, community non-profit organizations, the mayor, your city council, and perhaps even the Governor's office or your congressional representatives. Many times, power is shared by businesses, community groups, and the different levels of government.

Though the whole process may seem complex, one shortcut to figuring out who's got the power is to **follow the money trail.** Find out which government departments, agencies, or non-profit foundations are involved in the issue you are interested in and track down those that provide the dollars for operating expenses or enforcement. You may discover that a rundown neighborhood recreation center gets funds from the town council, several private sponsors, and the U.S. Department of Justice, or a school program is paid for by the board of education using local and state government money. This information often will lead you to the people who actually decide how money will be spent — specifically local, state and federal officials who have been elected by the voters and a number of other business and community leaders who care about what you think.

Politicians Are People, Too... So Get To Know Them!

It helps to know a bit about your audience before you talk with them. Calling the decision-maker's office or checking out his/her Web page will yield important biographical material (political party affiliation, profession, top legislative priorities, etc.). Personal info, such as where they graduated from high school, can help you mobilize students attending the same school who can play on this connection.

At a minimum, this background information will reveal that politicians are everyday individuals like you, and reduce feelings of intimidation or anxiety. More likely, you will be able to highlight a common interest, become friendly, and perhaps appeal to their sense of right and wrong. Ultimately, you want this decision-maker to feel obligated to give serious consideration to your effort.

YOUTH!

LEADERS AT THE DIFFERENT LEVELS

LOCAL GOVERNMENT

CITY, TOWN:
Mayor
City or town manager
Your council member, commissioner, alderman, supervisor etc.
Youth advisory council *

COUNTY, PARISH:
County Executive
Your county council member, commissioner, supervisor, etc.
Youth advisory commission *

SCHOOL DISTRICT:
Your school board member
At-Large school board members
Student board member(s) *
Superintendent *

STATE GOVERNMENT
Governor
Lieutenant Governor
Speaker of the House
President of the Senate
House and Senate Minority Leaders
Your state senator(s)
Your state representative(s)
Commissioner or Secretary of the State, Department of Health, Department of Education, Department of Environment, etc. *

NATIONAL GOVERNMENT
President
Vice President (also President of the Senate)
Senate Majority Leader
Speaker of the House of Representatives
House and Senate Minority Leaders
Your two U.S. senators
Your U.S. representative(s)
Secretary of the Department of Education, Environmental Protection Agency, Defense Department, and other agencies *
U.S. Surgeon General, Attorney General, FBI Director, etc. *

NON-PROFIT ORGANIZATIONS AND FOUNDATIONS
President
Executive Officers
Members of the Board of Directors
Members/Staff

COMPANIES AND BUSINESSES
Chief Executive Officer (CEO)
President & Executive Officers
Members of the Board of Directors
Stockholders
Managers/Employees

* usually appointed, not elected

These people can help you trace the money supply since they may be the ones who voted for the programs in the first place. They will want to know how the programs have benefited you (or how they haven't) and if you think the money is being spent wisely or if it is being misused. Your ideas on how funds should be spent will interest them because they want to get more "bang for the buck." Talk to them and their staff.

In addition they can usually **pinpoint the key person** you should contact at the school district's central office, the transportation department, environmental agency, non-profit community organization, etc., in order to get more information. They will also be able to tell you whether the local government has the authority over an issue or if your state legislature has to give the green light first.

In addition to adults, your peers may hold positions of power and be insiders themselves. Many local and state school boards now have student members, some of whom have voting rights *(more about this on pages 84-88)*. Youth may be participating as members of citizen boards (such as the Mayor's Youth Advisory Council, Parks and Recreation Teen Planning Board, or the Lieutenant Governor's Substance Abuse Task Force), and also be serving on the board of directors of community groups and foundations (such as Youth As Resources and the National 4-H). These youth members are likely to have lots of connections themselves and be willing to help you out.

26% at work — YOUTH ON THE INSIDE TRACK . . .

The Board of Young Adult Police Commissioners, composed of students from area high schools, advises city officials on proposed curfews, interviews new police recruits, and advocates ways in which police and other government agencies can better improve relations with youth in New Haven, Connecticut.

The San Francisco Youth Commission consists of 17 members between the ages of 12 and 23 who represent a number of different neighborhoods and diverse backgrounds. Any legislation pertaining to young people must be given to the Youth Commission to review and make recommendations prior to passage by the San Francisco Board of Supervisors.

YOUTH!

Since responsibility for many issues can be shared by a number of different power-holders, you may be faced with redefining what impact you want to have or choosing which audience is the best to target. Consider whether you want to affect only your immediate community or the whole state. Will you have the resources? Are there any obstacles? Who is more likely to approve your idea? If the change you are seeking requires approval by the state legislature, think about whether you have the time, money, energy, and ability to mobilize enough people across the state, as well as money, to mount a campaign that may also involve travel to the state capitol. Weigh your options and see which one is best for you, your team, and, ultimately, what you are trying to achieve.

SETTING GOALS
AND A GAME PLAN

After researching a little more about your issue and, of course, deciding whom you will need to convince, it is likely that you will have revised your solution a number of times. That's normal and to be expected. However, at a certain point, you and your team will need to translate your solution into action and decide what your goals are and how you wish to achieve them.

Your campaign may require a variety of **action plans:** organizing a letter-writing campaign, producing a public service announcement, testifying before a legislative committee or planning a youth summit. You might get results quickly but usually expect a sustained effort lasting weeks, months or even longer. You may also have to use a combination of tactics, approaching different audiences from different angles at different times. So be prepared and don't limit any of your options.

You will probably be eager to start. Before you do, **make sure your team is heading in the same direction.** Spend some time together defining your goals. A mission statement declaring your vision will make it easier for the group to agree on a plan of action. One approach is to have everyone contribute a phrase, single sentence or paragraph. Then one or two people can draft a statement to be reviewed and finalized by the whole team. Some mission statements can be used as the basis of organizational platforms, formal recommendations, speeches, news releases, and requests for donations.

PUT IT IN WRITING: MISSION STATEMENT

The following mission statement is taken from Staten Island Citizens Against (SICA) Graffiti (pronounced "sick-a'-graffiti"), a group of New York high school students and teachers.

MISSION STATEMENT

The primary objective behind our campaign is to educate all of Staten Island to the fact that graffiti vandalism is not some cutesy art form or harmless prank, but a deliberate criminal act. When you deface and destroy public and private property, you're committing a crime. The SICA Graffiti campaign hopes to promote awareness of the problem through an educational program that prompts students and teachers to take action to find a solution. The founders of SICA Graffiti firmly believe that each individual can make a difference, and when enough people voice their disgust with graffiti vandalism, the problem will decline significantly.

This one paragraph document printed on the group's letterhead helped enlist the support of other schools, community leaders, and local businesses. Many merchants and organizations collaborated with the students' "Adopt a Wall" program, resulting in 500 graffiti-free locations.

A game plan begins to take shape once a **"to do" list** is compiled. Make sure all activities support your goal and will help you achieve your mission. Use a big calendar with dates marked out for final exams, spring break and other major events. Then discuss as a group when certain tasks need to be done. If you are planning to meet with your city

YOUTH!

HINT: PICKING UP THE PACE

Here's one early team activity that is sure to get everyone involved, build momentum, and get your campaign noticed. A few people in your group can draft a news release announcing the formation of your group and send it off to the school and local newspapers. Several others can start a survey of about 10 students at each middle or high school in your area. The survey should reveal what students think about certain programs or policies. This type of one- or two-week activity serves as a test run to see each individual's strengths and interests and how well everyone can work as a team. Also, you are likely to achieve some concrete accomplishments: The survey may help to recruit new students to the team and can attract news coverage that will put your campaign on the map.

council or hold a press conference, one approach is to **set a date and plan backwards**. Then you can see if the date is realistic. Think about adding a couple of extra days or even weeks to your schedule to give everyone more leeway.

Also, strive to divide up the work by **delegating responsibilities** so the burden does not fall too heavily on only a few people. You might choose to leave it to each team member to pick a task according to his or her own talents and interests. Sometimes it will be necessary to coax several individuals to fill certain slots. Encouraging reluctant team players to work in pairs or form a subcommittee can make it more fun and appealing. In addition, it's wise to write down what everyone volunteers to do and the projected completion date, and give everyone a copy. **This defines what the expectations are and reinforces the importance of every team member following through.**

ACTION PLAN

Outline strategies/action steps for each identified goal and its objectives. <u>Objectives to be achieved: 1)</u>
Develop a district-wide policy promoting a tobacco-free environment for Emporia United School District 253.

ACTIONS What needs to be done?	BY WHOM Who will take action?	BY WHEN By what date will action be done?	RESOURCES/SUPPORT NEEDED/AVAILABLE What financial, human, political, & other resources are needed? What resources are *available*?	POTENTIAL BARRIERS or RESISTANCE What individuals and/or organizations might resist? How?	COMMUNICATION What organizations need to be informed about the actions?
Present concept of tobacco-free school grounds to High School teachers and staff	High School	11/14/96	High School Administration	Teachers, employees, parents who are anti-regulation	School Board
Survey USD 253 students and staff for opinions on tobacco-free policy	USD Admin., & high school students	11/22/96	High School Office Staff (making copies)	same	same as above
Research other USD policies	Admin. & HS students		school/USD office staff, other school districts	none	same as above
Draft tobacco-free school grounds policy	USD Admin., & high school students	1/31/97	USD staff, HS staff	School Board members	School Board
Educate USD 253 employees & students re: harmful effects of ETS	Lyon County Health Dept., HS students	ongoing	Health Dept. staff, HS students	Teachers, parents	same as above
Propose tobacco-free policy to USD 253 School Board for adoption	HS students, Tobacco Free Schools Coalition	2/28/97	HS students, administration	School Board members, parents of students	same as above
Hold tobacco cessation classes for USD 253 employees and	Lyon County Health Dept.	5/16/97	Health Department staff	none	HS students, USD 253 staff

This student-led campaign in Kansas resulted in a new school policy!

YOUTH!

ACTION PLANNING POINTERS

1 Make sure contact information is listed for the person in charge of keeping tabs and following the individual progress of members.

2 List the estimated schedule or timeline of all events. You may have to make a more detailed schedule for each event with deadlines or milestones and include that with the game plan.

3 Divide up assignments so individual members or pairs of people have responsibility for short-term tasks (Web page design, compiling survey results, etc.).

4 Include a system for providing regular updates and making sure everybody on the team receives information.

Regular communication between members is essential. It's great if one person volunteers to take on this responsibility. **Phone calls** can help move tasks to completion. On-line chats can even be a substitute for meetings and speed things along, provided that everyone has access to participate. Let your teammates know about any progress via telephone tree or sending out e-mail messages.

As things get rolling, you and your team might notice that things don't always happen as you had planned. Expect to hit **obstacles,** whether they come from decision-makers or even members of your own group. For instance, someone might not follow through or your team could get side-tracked by other issues. **Try to understand the situation** and provide support and enthusiasm whenever you can. Keep your teammates on task and work through problems as a group. These trying times and experiences only make you stronger, wiser, and more capable in the future.

One way to deal with situations that might arise is to try to predict them before they actually happen. Sit down with your team and **come up with a list of all the things that could possibly go wrong.** Anticipate everything from what happens if someone gets sick to if your principal refuses to grant permission for you to hold an assembly. Decide how your group wants to handle the problem. Devise a plan and practice. Then, if something unexpected happens, you'll be all the more ready to deal with it. If it doesn't, just consider yourselves lucky.

Of course, **not all surprises are going to be bad**. You could be invited to speak at a conference or your team could be highlighted for their efforts on the evening news. Take it all in stride and share the glory. You might have to change your timetable and experiment with different approaches. Just keep your sights on the goal and you'll do fine!

A NATIONAL CAMPAIGN THAT STARTED SMALL AND GREW!

William Wong, who at the age of 11 won the Eco-Inventor Award for his solar car design, helped develop a national bicycling campaign to reduce automobile use and air pollution. As a member of the Earth Force Youth Advisory Board, William's first step was to convince his principal to re-install bike racks that had been removed years ago. When his principal refused, William and members of his high school bike club started a petition and eventually got their principal to change his mind. In addition, William has worked to plan a "Bike Day" in San Francisco to coincide with similar events in other cities across the country. His long-term environmental plan of action consists of raising public awareness and convincing decision-makers to put more money into bike lanes and trails.

$EEKING $UPPORT

Certain types of campaigns will cost money in order to get off the ground or stay in motion. Just think about all the things you'll need — posters, printers, copiers, a phone, maybe even office space — and don't forget about the small stuff either, like paper, envelopes, postage, etc. Expenses can easily exceed what you and your group can pay for personally, so come up with a budget and estimate how much money your campaign will cost and what you can afford. Failure to consider your financial needs may limit what you are able to do, sometimes while the campaign is in full gear. See if a few resourceful members of your team are willing to take the lead on seeking money as well as free services and other non-cash donations.

HERE ARE A FEW RECOMMENDATIONS TO GET YOU STARTED:

MAKE A GOOD FIRST IMPRESSION.

If you make a written request for a financial contribution from an organization, then use your official campaign letterhead and include your mission statement. When attending meetings or conferences, be ready to pass out handouts, including any newspaper articles about your initiative and what you hope to accomplish.

BE DIRECT, BE SPECIFIC.

If you are invited to speak to a business or community organization, don't be shy about asking for support in terms of dollars and technical assistance. Some generous folks want to know how you're going to spend the money they're giving to you. Getting the word out about certain projects will motivate others to donate, such as $250 to pay for a Web page or for a bus to transport students to the state capitol.

START SMALL.

Consider traditional fundraising methods like car washes and raffles before planning major events such as an auction or concert that can divert most of your energy away from the cause itself. While washing cars or selling cupcakes, you can use this opportunity to get more than money. Share information about your campaign and try to turn others into activists, perhaps by asking them to sign a petition or pledge card.

ASK FOR IN-KIND DONATIONS.

Instead of asking for cold, hard cash, investigate whether local businesses would be willing to

PENNIES FOR A MONUMENTAL DIFFERENCE

High school students in Arizona successfully raised enough pennies to realize their dream: placing a bronze plaque at the Lincoln Memorial in Washington, D.C., where Martin Luther King, Jr., delivered his "I Have A Dream Speech."

STUDENTS MAKE $ENSE

At busy intersections in Chicago, "canning" brings in thousands of dollars to pay for the office rent and other expenses of the Student Alliance. A city solicitor's permit and the organization's insurance policy covers this "no strings attached" fund-raising operation and the students who do the "canning" earn an hourly wage.

OPERATION:

RESPONSIBLE ACTION FOR A VERY IMPORTANT NEIGHBORHOOD ECOSYSTEM

THE PROBLEM SOLVERS AND EARTH CLUB OF ELM PLACE MIDDLE SCHOOL PRESENT "CELEBRITY TRASH AUCTION"

HELLER NATURE CENTER
HIGHLAND PARK, IL
APRIL 24TH, 1994   3-5 P.M.

AUCTION ITEMS

1. WILL VINTON STUDIOS
Claymation Hotel sign from California Raisin
Monster Xerox Designs
Signed Letter
Foam Pumpkin
Photo-Cells
2. BIG BIRD SESAME STREET
Big Bird Photo door sign and more with love from your
feathered friend.
3. ELLEN CONFORS (CHILDREN'S AUTHOR)
This children's author's discarded manuscript papers,
personal message, scrabble notes.
4. WEIRD AL YANKOVIC
Weird Al tore this letter up and sent it back as his
trash.
5. DUDLEY MOORE
Signed crushed Diet Pepsi can.

Signed cocktail
53. MICHAEL CRICHTON
Signed Jurassic Park postcard.
54. RICHARD LEDERER (AUTHOR)
Signed book, "The Miracle of Language."
55. MADELINE L'ENGLE (AUTHOR)
Signed fabric square
Signed letter

creative guidance of
Susie Greenwald are to be commended for
making this project a success. We would like to remind
you that proceeds from this fundraiser will go to
restore the ravine adjacent to Elm Place Middle School
in Highland Park, IL.

provide you with office equipment such as a photocopier or postage meter. In addition to products, inquire about donated services. A printer, if asked and convinced about your good work, may be delighted to make business cards or posters for you for free or at a reduced cost.

NO TAX-EXEMPT STATUS...NO PROBLEM.

Individuals and businesses often don't want to make a contribution unless they receive a tax deduction. Provided that your campaign does not work on behalf of political parties or candidates, you can usually find a non-profit community organization willing to become your official fiscal agent. That means those giving you money can write-off their donations. If your organization expects to hire staff and go "big time," find a lawyer who will donate his/her services to help you apply to the Internal Revenue Service (IRS) for tax-exempt status (the lingo is "501(c)(3)," which refers to the section of the tax code you're interested in).

TRACK DOWN MINI-GRANT$.

Ask around and you're likely to discover a community organization or local government agency that gives away money, usually between $500 to $5000, for a variety of projects. Private, non-

YOUTH!

APPLICATION FORM & GUIDELINES
ROBINSON MINI-GRANT PROGRAM FOR K-12 SERVICE LEARNING
Sponsored by the Constitutional Rights Foundation
DEADLINE: JUNE 2, 1997

Name of Project ___For The Children___

Grade(s) & School Subjects Involved ___K-12___

School Name & Address (include state) ___Scotia-Glenville High School, iTartan Way, Scotia, New York 12302___ ___middle schools in Troy + Scotia + elementary schools in Albany + Scotia___

School Phone (_518_) _382-1231_   Fax (_518_) _382-1215_

Teacher Sponsor (please print) ___Jean B. Rose___

Signature of Teacher Sponsor ___Jean B. Rose___

Summer Contact: Name & Address ___835 Lakewood Avenue, Schenectady, New York 12309___

Student Planners ___Francesca Cichello, Rag Ciervo, Alison Gifford___

School Congressional Representative _____

Amount of Grant $ _575_ . (Remember, the ma[x]
a grant are higher if you request less than $600.)

EXCERPT FROM MINI-GRANT PROPOSAL THAT GOT $$$

ROBINSON MINI-GRAN[T]
K-12 SERVICE LEARN[ING]

GIVE COLLABORATION:
SCOTIA-GLENVILLE CENTRAL SCHOOLS

Project Highlights

▷ **Diversity** (Bringing K-12 suburban and urban students of all abilities together to work for common cause)
▷ **Health** (Teaching parenting skills)
▷ **Violence Prevention** (Teaching Child Abuse Awareness/Prevention)
▷ **Matching Funds** (Support from community organizations)

1) **Community Need**

More than 7,000 children are abused or neglected in this country everyday. Experts estimate that 1,400 boys and girls will die from abuse and neglect in 1997. Statistical data and pedagogical research substantiate the need for broad based training for all citizens in this country. We can not begin too early to teach children the critical importance of responsible, skilled knowledgeable parenting.

[S is a su]____[urban servi]___[aming ce]____ of four sc[hool] [distric]____ [Glenvi]___

profit organizations such as the Ryan White Foundation or Youth As Resources offer mini-grants for programs that are designed and carried out by young people. Many government agencies such as your county health department provide funds to students with a plan to reduce teen smoking or substance abuse. The application may be a simple one-page form. In other cases, an oral presentation is necessary in addition to a more lengthy written proposal.

GRANT MONEY IS OUT THERE

High school sophomore Cassie Fuller was concerned that young people needed a safe place to hang out and have fun and got nearly $3,000 worth of grants to start the New Horizons Teen Center in her town. "I found out about grants through the 4-H and the South Carolina Drug and Alcohol Commission. They'd get the applications for me and tell me who to call, and I wrote the grant. The first grant came from the Bureau of Justice Assistance, Office of Drug Prevention in Washington, D.C., and that paid for tile we needed for the dance floor."

MAJOR GRANT OPPORTUNITIES.

Federal government agencies, such as the U.S. Environmental Protection Agency or the U.S. Department of Justice, give money to individual states to encourage local efforts to develop creative solutions to everyday problems. Your campaign may be eligible to get some of these funds. Other opportunities include philanthropic foundations and other private organizations that award grants. Most contributors have strict guidelines and do not award money to individuals; however, most schools, youth groups, and community organizations can compete. See if a local organization can suggest someone experienced in writing grant proposals to help you.

SOME GUIDELINES ON APPLYING FOR GRANTS . . .

If you are applying as a school club or group, most likely you will need the permission of your principal or another administrator. Sometimes, the Board of Education will have special policies concerning how student groups are allowed to use grant money. (To get around this obstacle, your group can become an independent organization separate from school).

Most applications are reviewed by a panel of judges chosen by the potential funder. They must be convinced your project is worthy. Besides describing the goals of your campaign, be sure to include supporting facts and statistics. Expect to be asked for a proposed budget and a procedure for evaluating your project.

Type your grant proposal. Ask someone to review your application and check for proper grammar and correct spelling. Mistakes can be embarrassing and may count against you when your application is being judged.

Try to get a **letter of support from an adult ally**, even if the grant application does not require it. It can give your application an edge and lend credibility to what you are trying to do.

YOUTH!

Some grants require matching funds. This means you will need to match every dollar that the grant provides with a dollar from somewhere else. Make sure your group will be able to raise the money. If you can't, you may risk losing the entire grant or being forced to pay back what you have already spent.

Federal grants will not usually be paid immediately. Several months may pass before a check arrives. If your organization is in need of money in a hurry, your best bet is to pursue local funds and individual donations.

Be sure to keep receipts and records of expenses and everything related to your overall budget. Keep it organized. Also, be sure to thank your contributors. Along with letters expressing appreciation to any individual, organization or company that has helped you along the way, include a summary of accomplishments, perhaps even a videotape showing footage of a youth summit or a TV story profiling the campaign. This concrete evidence of your ongoing work will increase the likelihood of getting additional support from these same people and organizations in the future.

  RAISING $

(Also refer to the next section: Over 100 National Organizations and Clearinghouses)

CATALOG OF FEDERAL DOMESTIC ASSISTANCE
US General Services Administration
300 Seventh Street SW
Washington DC 20407
202-708-5126
www.gsa.gov/fdac
The Catalog, available at many public and university libraries, identifies thousands of grants made by dozens of federal government agencies.

CENTER FOR YOUTH AS RESOURCES
1000 Connecticut Ave.
Washington DC 20006
202-466-6272
www.yar.org
YAR programs are governed by local boards of youth and adults that provide small grants for positive community change projects designed by people age 5 to 21.

DO SOMETHING
423 W. 55th Street 8th Floor
New York NY 10019
212-523-1175
www.dosomething.org
This national organization offers $500 grants to people under 30 for youth-oriented community projects.

THE FOUNDATION CENTER
79 Fifth Avenue
New York NY 10013
800-424-9836
www.fdncenter.org
This private clearinghouse has resources to help identify corporate, philanthropic and government funding sources.

IRS EXEMPT ORGANIZATIONS TECHNICAL DIVISION
U.S. Department of the Treasury
1111 Constitution Avenue NW
#6411
Washington DC 20224
202-622-8100
The Internal Revenue Service or your local IRS office has forms and free help available on applying for tax-exempt status.

OVER 100 NATIONAL ORGANIZATIONS AND CLEARINGHOUSES

This list is by no means meant to be complete — only a **starting point to help you with your research and fundraising efforts**. Each organization and clearinghouse can refer you to many other national non-profit and government agencies and also identify local groups in your own hometown. Some well-known associations, such as the Audubon Society, PTA, Teen Institute, and YMCA, are not included because you should be able to locate nearby chapters by looking in your local telephone book. Other organizations have been listed elsewhere in this handbook, under the heading of INFO-STARTERS. For all the organizations that are listed under different subject categories, **keep in mind that telephone numbers and addresses change** as frequently as the weather. An e-mail address is included for those organizations without a Web site. Good luck!

1st—GENERAL
Abortion (see Sexuality)
Abstinence (see Sexuality)
ADVERTISING
AIDS (see Sexuality)
ALCOHOL/DRUGS
ANIMALS
BIKES/CARS/TRANSPORTATION
Censorship (see Constitutional Rights)
CHILD ABUSE
Civil Rights (see Constitutional Rights; Discrimination/Racism)
College (see Student Loans; Community Service/Volunteerism)
COMMUNITY SERVICE/VOLUNTEERISM
Computers (see Education/Schools; Internet)
CONSTITUTIONAL RIGHTS
CONSUMER PROTECTION
CRIME/VIOLENCE PREVENTION
Date Rape (see Crime/Violence Prevention; Sexuality)
DISCRIMINATION/RACISM
Driver's License (see Bikes/Cars/Transportation)

Dropout Prevention (see Education/Schools)
Drugs (see Alcohol/Drugs; Tobacco)
Drunk Driving (see Bikes/Cars/Transportation)
EATING DISORDERS/NUTRITION
EDUCATION/SCHOOLS
ELECTIONS/CAMPAIGN FINANCE
EMPLOYMENT/JOBS
Entrepreneurship (see Employment/Jobs)
ENVIRONMENT
FAMILIES/PARENTING
Gangs (see Crime/Violence Prevention)
Gay & Lesbian (see Discrimination/Racism; Sexuality; Suicide/Depression)
Global Warming (see Environment)
Government (see Chapter 4)
Graffiti (see Crime/Violence Prevention)
Guns (see Crime/Violence Prevention)
Health (see 1st—General; Alcohol/Drugs; Crime/Violence Prevention; Sexuality; Suicide/Depression; Tobacco)
Health Curriculum (see Education/Schools; Sexuality)
HIV (see Sexuality)

HOMELESSNESS/HUNGER

Homicide (see Crime/Violence Prevention)

Homophobia (see Discrimination/Racism)

Human Rights (see International)

IMMIGRATION

INTERNATIONAL

INTERNET

Mental Health (see 1st—General; Homelessness/Hunger; Suicide/Depression)

Multiculturalism/Diversity (see Discrimination/Racism; Education/Schools)

NEIGHBORHOOD IMPROVEMENT

Parenting (see Child Abuse; Families/Parenting)

Population (see International)

Poverty (see Homelessness/Hunger; International)

Pregnancy (see Sexuality)

Prejudice (see Discrimination/Racism)

Racism (see Discrimination/Racism)

Rainforests (see Environment)

Rape (see Crime/Violence Prevention)

Recycling (see Environment)

RELIGION

Safety (see Bikes/Cars/Transportation; Crime/Violence Prevention)

Schools (see Education/Schools)

Sexual Harassment (see Discrimination/Racism; Education/Schools)

Sexism (see Discrimination/Racism)

SEXUALITY

Smoking (see Tobacco)

SPORTS & EXERCISE

STDs (see Sexuality)

Stereotypes (see Discrimination/Racism)

Stress (see Suicide/Depression)

STUDENT LOANS

Students & Student Rights (see Constitutional Rights; Education/Schools; Student Loans)

SUICIDE/DEPRESSION

Technology (see Education/Schools; Internet)

Teen Parents (see Families/Parenting)

TOBACCO

Traffic (see Bikes/Cars/Transportation)

TV/MOVIES

Video Games (see Constitutional Rights; Internet; TV/Movies)

Violence (see Crime/Violence Prevention)

Volunteerism (see Community Service/Volunteerism)

Voting (see Elections/Campaign Finance)

1st—GENERAL

AMERICAN YOUTH POLICY FORUM
1836 Jefferson Place
Washington DC 20036
202-775-9731
www.aypf.org

CENTER FOR YOUTH DEVELOPMENT AND POLICY RESEARCH
1875 Connecticut Avenue NW
Washington DC 20009
202-884-8267
www.aed.org

CHILDREN NOW
1212 Broadway #530
Oakland CA 94612
510-763-2444
www.childrennow.org

NATIONAL ASSEMBLY
National Collaboration for Youth
1319 F Street NW #601
Washington DC 20004
202-347-2080
www.assembly.org

NATIONAL CLEARINGHOUSE FOR FAMILIES AND YOUTH
PO Box 13505
Silver Spring MD 20911
301-608-8098
www.acf.dhhs.gov/ncfy

NATIONAL ISSUES FORUM
Kettering Foundation
200 Commons Road
Dayton OH 45459
937-434-7300
www.kettering.org

NATIONAL NETWORK FOR YOUTH
1319 F Street NW #401
Washington DC 20004
800-878-2437
www.NN4Youth.org

STUDY CIRCLES RESOURCE CENTER
PO Box 203
Pomfret CT 06258
860-928-2616
scrc@neca.com

YOUTHINFO
U.S. Department of Health and Human Services

200 Independence Avenue SW #405G
Washington DC 20201
202-690-5937
youth.os.dhhs.gov

ADVERTISING

(see also Consumer Protection; Internet; TV/Movies)

ACCURACY IN THE MEDIA
1275 K Street NW
Washington DC 20005
202-371-6710
www.aim.org

BERKELEY MEDIA STUDIES GROUP
2140 Shattuck Avenue #804
Berkeley CA 94704
510-204-9700
bmsg@bsmg.org

CAMPAIGN FOR COMMERCIAL-FREE PUBLIC EDUCATION
360 Grand Avenue #385
Oakland CA 94610
800-UNPLUG-1
unplug@igc.org

CENTER FOR MEDIA
EDUCATION
1511 K Street NW
Washington DC 20036
202-628-2620
www.cme.org

CENTER FOR THE STUDY OF
COMMERCIALISM
1875 Connecticut Avenue
Washington DC 20009
202-332-9110
www.cspinet.org

NATIONAL ASSOCIATION OF
AFRICAN AMERICANS FOR
POSITIVE IMAGERY
3536 North 16th Street
Philadelphia PA 19140
215-225-5232
naappi@msn.com

U.S. FEDERAL TRADE
COMMISSION
Sixth and Pennsylvania Avenue NW
Washington DC 20580
202-326-3131
www.ftc.gov

ALCOHOL/DRUGS
(see also Tobacco; Education;
Crime/Violence Prevention;
Bikes/Cars/Transportation;
Neighborhood Improvement)

CENTER FOR SUBSTANCE
ABUSE TREATMENT
5600 Fishers Lane
Rockville MD 20857
301-443-5700
www.samhsa.gov/csat

COMMUNITY ANTI-DRUG
COALITIONS OF AMERICA
901 North Pitt Street #300
Alexandria VA 22314
703-706-0560
www.cadca.org

DRUG POLICY FOUNDATION
4455 Connecticut Avenue
Washington DC 20008
202-537-5005
www.dpf.org

DRUG STRATEGIES
2445 M Street
Washington DC 20037
202-663-6090
www.drugstrategies.org

JOIN TOGETHER
1 Stuart Street
Boston MA 02166
617-437-1500
www.jointogether.org

MARIN INSTITUTE FOR THE
PREVENTION OF ALCOHOL
AND OTHER DRUG
PROBLEMS
24 Belvedere Street
San Rafael CA 94901
415-456-5692
www.marininstitute.org

NATIONAL ASSOCIATION OF
STATE ALCOHOL AND DRUG
ABUSE DIRECTORS
808 17th Street NW
Washington DC 20006
202-293-0090
www.nasadad.org

NATIONAL CLEARINGHOUSE
FOR ALCOHOL AND DRUG
INFORMATION
PO Box 2345
Rockville MD 20847
800-729-6686
www.health.org

NATIONAL INSTITUTE ON
ALCOHOL ABUSE AND
ALCOHOLISM
PO Box 10686
Rockville MD 20849
Tel: N/A Fax: 202-842-0418
www.niaaa.nih.gov

NATIONAL INSTITUTE ON
DRUG ABUSE
5600 Fishers Lane Room 10-A39
Rockville MD 20857
301-443-1124
www.nida.nih.gov

NATIONAL INHALANTS
PREVENTION COALITION
1201 West 6th Street
Austin TX 78703
800-269-4237
www.inhalants.org

STUDENTS AGAINST
DESTRUCTIVE DECISIONS
(SADD)
Box 800
Marlboro MA 01752
508-481-3568
www.nat-sadd.org

ANIMALS
(see also Environment; International)

AMERICAN SOCIETY FOR THE
PREVENTION OF CRUELTY TO
ANIMALS
441 East 92nd Street
New York NY 10128
212-876-7000
www.aspca.org

ANIMAL WELFARE
INFORMATION CENTER
National Agricultural Library #304
Beltsville MD 20705
301-504-6212
www.nalusda.gov/answers

CENTER FOR MARINE
CONSERVATION
1725 DeSales Street NW
Washington DC 20006
202-429-5609
www.cmc-ocean.org

HUMANE SOCIETY OF THE U.S.
2100 L Street NW
Washington DC 20037
202-452-1100
www.hsus.org

NATIONAL ANTI-VIVISECTION
SOCIETY
53 West Jackson Blvd #1550
Chicago IL 60604
312-427-6065
www.quikpage.com/N/natlantivi

NATIONAL WILDLIFE
FEDERATION
9825 Leesburg Pike
Vienna VA 22184
703-979-3000
www.nwf.org

PEOPLE FOR THE ETHICAL
TREATMENT OF ANIMALS
PO Box 42516
Washington DC 20015
301-770-PETA
www.peta-online.org

U.S. FISH AND WILDLIFE
SERVICE
4401 North Fairfax Drive
Arlington VA 22203
703-358-1711
www.fws.gov

BIKES/CARS/
TRANSPORTATION
(see also Alcohol/Drugs; Consumer
Protection; Environment)

ADVOCATES FOR HIGHWAY
AND AUTO SAFETY
750 First Street NE
Washington DC 20002
202-408-1711
www.saferoads.org

BICYCLE FEDERATION OF
AMERICA
1506 21st Street NW
Washington DC 20036
202-463-6622
www.bikefed.org

MOTHERS AGAINST DRUNK
DRIVING
511 East John Carpenter Freeway
Irving TX 75062
800-GET-MADD
www.madd.org

NATIONAL COMMITTEE FOR
UNIFORM TRAFFIC LAWS
AND ORDINANCES
405 Church Street
Evanston IL 60204
800-323-4011
www.ncutlo.org

NATIONAL HIGHWAY TRAFFIC
SAFETY ADMINISTRATION
U.S. Department of Transportation
400 Seventh Street SW NTS-21
Washington DC 20590
202-366-9588
www.nhtsa.dot.gov

NATIONAL SAFETY COUNCIL
1121 Spring Lake Drive
Itasca IL 60143
800-621-7619
www.nsc.org

YOUTH!

NATIONAL SCHOOL
TRANSPORTATION
ASSOCIATION
PO Box 2639
Springfield VA 22152
703-644-0700
www.schooltrans.com

NATIONAL STUDENT SAFETY
PROGRAM
American Driver and Traffic Safety
Association
IUP Highway Safety Center
Indiana PA 15705
800-896-7703
adtsea.iup.edu/adtsea

CHILD ABUSE
(see also Families/Parenting;
Crime/Violence Prevention)

AMERICAN BAR
ASSOCIATION
Center on Children and the Law
740 15th St NW
Washington DC 20005
202-662-1720
www.abanet.org/child

FAMILY VIOLENCE
PREVENTION FUND
383 Rhode Island Street
San Francisco CA 94103
800-777-1960
www.fvpf.org

NATIONAL CHILD RIGHTS
ALLIANCE
PO Box 61125
Durham NC 27705
919-682-5509
jimsenter@delphi.com

NATIONAL CLEARINGHOUSE
FOR CHILD ABUSE AND
NEGLECT INFORMATION
PO Box 1182
Washington DC 20013
800-FYI-3366
www.calib.com/nccanch

NATIONAL RUNAWAY
SWITCHBOARD
3080 North Lincoln Avenue
Chicago IL 60657
800-344-2785
www.nrscrisisline.org

COMMUNITY
SERVICE/
VOLUNTEERISM
(see also Education; Neighborhood
Improvement)

AMERICA'S PROMISE
909 North Washington Street
Alexandria VA 22314
703-684-4500
www.americas-promise.org

CAMPUS OUTREACH
OPPORTUNITY LEAGUE
1511 K Street NW
Washington DC 20005
202-637-7004
www.cool2serve.org

AMERICORPS/
LEARN AND SERVE
Corporation for National Service
1201 New York Avenue NW
Washington DC 20525
202-606-5000 ext 135
www.cns.gov/learn

INDEPENDENT SECTOR
1828 L Street
Washington DC 20036
202-223-8100
www.indepsec.org

NATIONAL SERVICE-
LEARNING COOPERATIVE
CLEARINGHOUSE
University of Minnesota
1954 Buford Avenue R-290
St. Paul MN 55108
800-808-7378
www.nicsl.coled.umn.edu

NATIONAL YOUTH
LEADERSHIP COUNCIL
1910 W. County Road B
Roseville MN 55113
800-366-6952
nylc.org

POINTS OF LIGHT
FOUNDATION
1400 Eye N.W.
Washington DC 20005
202-729-8000
www.pointsoflight.org

YMCA EARTH SERVICE CORPS
909 Fourth Avenue
Seattle WA 98104
800-733-YESC
www.yesc.org

YOUTH SERVICE AMERICA
1101 15th Street NW
Washington DC 20005
202-296-2992
www.servenet.org/ysanet2

CONSTITUTIONAL
RIGHTS
(see also Discrimination/Racism;
Internet)

AMERICAN BAR
ASSOCIATION
Special Committee on Youth
Education and Citizenship
541 N. Fairbanks Court
Chicago IL 60611
312-988-5735
www.abanet.org

AMERICAN CENTER FOR LAW
AND JUSTICE
PO Box 64429
Virginia Beach VA 23467
757-579-2489
www.aclj.org

AMERICAN CIVIL LIBERTIES
UNION
132 West 43rd Street
New York NY 10036
212-944-9800
www.aclu.org

CENTER FOR DEMOCRATIC
RENEWAL
PO Box 50469
Atlanta GA 30302
404-221-0025
www.publiceye.org/pra/cdr

CONSTITUTIONAL RIGHTS
FOUNDATION
601 South Kingsley Drive
Los Angeles CA 90005
213-487-5590
www.crf-usa.org

FIRST AMENDMENT PROJECT
1736 Franklin Street
Oakland CA 94612
510-208-7744
www.well.com/user/fap

FREEDOM FORUM
1101 Wilson Blvd
Arlington VA 22209
703-528-0800
www.freedomforum.org

NATIONAL ORGANIZATION
FOR WOMEN
1000 16th Street
Washington DC 20036
202-331-0066
www.now.org

SECOND AMENDMENT
FOUNDATION
12500 NE 10th Place
Bellevue WA 98005
800-426-4302
www.saf.org

STREET LAW
918 16th Street
Washington DC 20006
202-293-0088
www.streetlaw.org

STUDENT PRESS LAW
CENTER
1101 Wilson Blvd
Arlington VA 22209
703-807-1904
www.splc.org

CONSUMER
PROTECTION
(see also Advertising;
Bikes/Cars/Transportation;
also refer to page 97)

CONSUMERS UNION
101 Truman Avenue
Yonkers NY 10703
914-378-2000
www.consumer.org

NATIONAL CONSUMERS
LEAGUE
1701 K Street NW
Washington DC 20006
202-835-3323
www.natlconsumersleague.org

NATIONAL FRAUD INSTITUTE
PO Box 65868
Washington DC 20035
800-876-7060
www.fraud.org

U.S. CONSUMER
PROTECTION SAFETY
COMMISSION
5401 Westbard Avenue
Washington DC 20207
800-638-2772
www.cpsc.gov

U.S. PUBLIC INTEREST
RESEARCH GROUP
218 D Street SE
Washington DC 20003
202-546-9707
www.pirg.org

CRIME/VIOLENCE PREVENTION

(see also Alcohol/Drugs; Child Abuse;
Constitutional Rights;
Education/Schools; Neighborhood
Improvement)

CENTER FOR YOUTH AS
RESOURCES
1000 Connecticut Ave.
Washington DC 20006
202-466-6272
www.yar.org

COMMUNITY POLICING
CONSORTIUM
1726 M Street NW
Washington DC 20036
800-833-3085
www.communitypolicing.org

CONFLICT RESOLUTION
UNLIMITED
845 106th Avenue NE
Bellevue WA 98004
800-922-1988
www.conflictnet.org/cru

EDUCATIONAL FUND TO END
HANDGUN VIOLENCE
1000 16th Street NW
Washington DC 20036
202-530-5888
www.gunfree.inter.net

INTERNATIONAL
ASSOCIATION OF CHIEFS OF
POLICE
515 North Washington Street
Alexandria VA 22314
800-THE-IACP
www.theiacp.org

JUVENILE JUSTICE
CLEARINGHOUSE
U.S. Department of Justice
1600 Research Blvd
Rockville MD 20850
800-638-8736
www.ncjrs.org

NATIONAL CENTER FOR
INJURY PREVENTION &
CONTROL
Centers for Disease Control
4770 Buford Highway NE
Atlanta GA 30341
770-488-4224
www.cdc.gov/ncipc

NATIONAL CRIME
PREVENTION COUNCIL
1000 Connecticut Ave.
Washington DC 2006
202-466-6272
www.ncpc.org

NATIONAL DOMESTIC
VIOLENCE HOTLINE
3616 Bar West #101-279
Austin TX 78731
800-799-SAFE
www.inetport.com/ndvh

NATIONAL RIFLE
ASSOCIATION
Institute for Legislative Action
1600 Rhode Island Avenue NW
Washington DC 20036
202-828-6000
www.nra.org

PARTNERSHIPS AGAINST
VIOLENCE ONLINE
10301 Baltimore Avenue #304
Beltsville MD 20705
301-504-5462
www.pavenet.org

RESOLVING CONFLICT
CREATIVELY PROGRAM
Educators for Social Responsibility
23 Garden Street
Cambridge MA 02138
617-492-1764
www.benjerry.com/esr

TEEN COURT PROGRAM
American Probation and Parole
Association
PO Box 11910
Lexington KY 40578
606-244-8215
www.csg.org/appa

YOUTH CRIME WATCH OF
AMERICA
9300 South Dadeland Blvd
Miami FL 33156
305-670-2409
www.ycwa.org

DISCRIMINATION/RACISM

(see also Constitutional Rights;
Education/Schools; Neighborhood
Improvement)

ANTI-DEFAMATION LEAGUE
823 United Nations Plaza
New York NY 10017
212-885-7774
www.adl.org

ARCHITECTURAL AND
TRANSPORTATION BARRIERS
COMPLIANCE BOARD
1331 F Street NW
Washington DC 20004
800-USA-ABLE
www.access-board.gov

ARTISTS FOR A HATE-FREE
AMERICA
800-3What2Do
www.hootie.com/ahfm

ASIAN-AMERICAN LEGAL
DEFENSE AND EDUCATION
FUND
99 Hudson Street
New York NY 10013
212-966-5932
aaldef@worldnet.att.net

ASPIRA ASSOCIATION, INC.
1444 Eye Street NW #800
Washington DC 20005
202-835-3600
www.incacorp.com/aspira

FACING HISTORY AND
OURSELVES
16 Hurd Street
Brookline MA 02146
617-232-1595
www.facing.org

GAY AND LESBIAN ALLIANCE
AGAINST DEFAMATION
1360 Mission Street
San Francisco CA 94103
415-861-2244
www.glaad.org

MUSLIM STUDENT NETWORK
974 Commercial Street
Palo Alto CA 94303
415-852-9052
www.mpac.org/msn

NATIONAL ASSOCIATION
FOR THE ADVANCEMENT OF
COLORED PEOPLE
4805 Hope Drive
Baltimore MD 21215
410-358-8900
www.naacp.org

NATIONAL INFORMATION
CENTER FOR CHILDREN AND
YOUTH WITH DISABILITIES
PO Box 1492
Washington DC 20013
202-884-8200
www.aed.org/nichcy

NATIONAL RAINBOW
COALITION
1002 Wisconsin Avenue NW
Washington DC 20007
202-333-5270

NATIVE AMERICAN RIGHTS
FUND
1506 Broadway
Boulder CO 80302
303-447-8760
www.narf.org

TEACHING TOLERANCE
Southern Poverty Law Center
400 Washington Avenue
Montgomery AL 36104
334-264-0286
www.splcenter.org

UNITED CHURCH OF CHRIST
COMMISSION FOR RACIAL
JUSTICE
700 Prospect Avenue East
Cleveland OH 44115
216-736-2168

YOUTH!

U.S. DEPARTMENT OF
JUSTICE
Community Relations Service
5550 Friendship Blvd
Chevy Chase MD 20815
800-547-HATE
www.doj.gov

EATING DISORDERS/
NUTRITION
(see Homelessness/Hunger)

AMERICAN
ANOREXIA/BULIMIA
ASSOCIATION
165 West 46th Street
New York NY 10036
212-575-6200
www.members.aol.com/AmAnBu

AMERICAN DIETETIC
ASSOCIATION
216 West Jackson Blvd
Chicago IL 60606
312-899-0040
www.eatright.org

AMERICAN SCHOOL FOOD
SERVICE ASSOCIATION
1600 Duke Street
Alexandria VA 22314
703-739-3900
www.asfsca.org

CENTER FOR NUTRITION
POLICY AND PROMOTION
US Department of Agriculture
1120 20th Street NW
Washington DC 20036
301-504-5719
www.usda.gov/fcs/cnpp

CENTER FOR SCIENCE IN THE
PUBLIC INTEREST
1875 Connecticut Avenue NW
Washington DC 20009
202-332-9110
www.cspinet.org

FOOD RESEARCH AND
ACTION CENTER
1875 Connecticut Avenue NW
Washington DC 20009
202-986-2200
www.frac.org

EDUCATION/SCHOOLS
(see also Community Service/
Volunteerism; Constitutional Rights;
Internet; Student Loans; Crime/
Violence Prevention; Alcohol/Drug
Abuse; also refer to page 88)

AMERICAN SCHOOL
COUNSELORS ASSOCIATION
801 North Fairfax
Alexandria VA 22314
800-306-4722
www.schoolcounselor.org

AMERICAN VOCATIONAL
ASSOCIATION
1410 King Street
Alexandria VA 22314
703-683-3111
www.avaonline.org

ASSOCIATION FOR
SUPERVISION AND
CURRICULUM DEVELOPMENT
1250 North Pitt
Alexandria VA 22314
703-549-9110
www.ascd.org

CENTER FOR SCHOOL
CHANGE
University of Minnesota
301 19th Avenue South
Minneapolis MN 55455
612-626-1834
www.hh.umn.edu/centers/school-
change

COMMUNITIES IN SCHOOLS
1199 N. Fairfax Street #300
Alexandria VA 22314
703-519-8999
www.cisnet.org

EDUCATIONAL RESOURCES
INFORMATION CENTER
U.S. Department of Education
2277 Research Blvd
Rockville MD 20850
800-CALL-ERIC
www.aspensys.com/eric

EDUCATION COMMISSION
OF THE STATES
707 17th Street
Denver CO 80202
303-299-3600
www.ecs.org

INTERNATIONAL STUDENT
ACTIVISM ALLIANCE
31 North Quaker Lane
West Hartford CT 06119
860-232-8452
www.studentactivism.org

NATIONAL ASSOCIATION OF
INDEPENDENT SCHOOLS
1601 L Street
Washington DC 20036
202-973-9700
www.nais-schools.org

NATIONAL ASSOCIATION OF
STATE BOARDS OF
EDUCATION
1012 Cameron Street
Alexandria VA 22314
703-684-4000
www.nasbe.org

NATIONAL ASSOCIATION OF
STUDENT COUNCILS
c/o National Association of Secondary
School Principals
1904 Association Drive
Reston VA 22091
703-860-0200 ext 336
www.nassp.org

NATIONAL DROPOUT
PREVENTION CENTER
Clemson University
205 Martin Street
Clemson SC 29634
800-656-2599
www.dropoutprevention.org

NATIONAL SCHOOL BOARDS
ASSOCIATION
1680 Duke Street
Alexandria VA 22314
703-838-6731
www.nsba.org

NATIONAL SCHOOL SAFETY
ASSOCIATION
4165 Thousand Oaks Blvd
Westlake CA 91362
805-373-9977
www.nssa1.org

SAFE AND DRUG-FREE
SCHOOLS
U.S. Department of Education
400 Maryland Ave SW #1073
Washington DC 20202
202-260-1856
www.ed.gov

ELECTIONS/
CAMPAIGN FINANCE
(see also page 82)

CENTER FOR VOTING AND
DEMOCRACY
PO Box 60037
Washington DC 20039
301-270-4616
www.igc.apc.org/cvd

CENTER FOR PUBLIC
INTEGRITY
1634 Eye Street NW
Washington DC 20006
202-783-3906
www.publicintegrity.org

COMMON CAUSE
1250 Connecticut Avenue NW
Washington DC 20036
202- 833-1200
www.commoncause.org

FEDERAL ELECTION
COMMISSION
999 E Street NW
Washington DC 20463
800-424-9530
www.fec.gov

FREE CONGRESS RESEARCH
AND EDUCATION
FOUNDATION
717 Second Street NW
Washington DC 20002
202-546-3000
www.fcref.org

PUBLIC CITIZEN
1600 20th Street NW
Washington DC 20009
202-588-1000
www.citizen.org

EMPLOYMENT/JOBS

AN INCOME OF HER OWN
1804 W. Burbank Blvd
Burbank CA 91506
800-350-2978
www.aioho.com

CENTER FOR
ENTREPRENEURIAL
LEADERSHIP
Kauffman Foundation
4900 Oak
Kansas City MO 64112
816-932-1000
www.emkf.org

CHILD LABOR COALITION
1701 K Street NW
Washington DC 20006
202-835-3323
www.natlconsumersleague.org/clc

FUTURE BUSINESS LEADERS
OF AMERICA
1912 Association Drive
Reston VA 20191
800-325-2946
www.fbla.org

NATIONAL FOUNDATION
FOR TEACHING
ENTREPRENEURSHIP
120 Wall Street 29th Floor
New York NY 10005
212-232-3333
www.pbs.org/jobs

NATIONAL URBAN LEAGUE
120 Wall Street
New York NY 10005
212-558-5300
www.nul.org

NATIONAL YOUTH
EMPLOYMENT COALITION
1001 Connecticut Avenue #728
Washington DC 20036
202-659-1064
www.ttrc.doleta.gov/pepnet

U.S. DEPARTMENT OF LABOR
Employment and Training
Administration
200 Constitution Avenue NW
Washington DC 20210
202-219-8550
www.ncjrs.org/appadol

U.S. EQUAL EMPLOYMENT
OPPORTUNITY COMMISSION
1801 L Street NW
Washington DC 20507
800-669-3362
www.eeoc.gov

YOUTHBUILD USA
PO Box 440322
Somerville MA 02144
617-623-9900
www. youthbuild.org

ENVIRONMENT
(see also Animals;
Bikes/Cars/Transportation;
International)

CONSERVATION AND
RENEWABLE ENERGY
INQUIRY AND REFERRAL
SERVICE
U.S. Department of Energy
PO Box 3048
Merrifield VA 22116

800-523-2929
www.eren.doe.gov

EARTH FORCE
1908 Mount Vernon Avenue
Alexandria VA 22301
703-299-9400
www.earthforce.org

ENVIRONMENTAL DEFENSE
FUND
257 Park Avenue South
New York NY 10010
212-505-2100
www.edf.org

GROUNDWATER
FOUNDATION
PO Box 22558
Lincoln NE 68542
800-858-4844
www.groundwater.org

ISAAK WALTON LEAGUE OF
AMERICA
707 Conservation Lane
Gaithersburg MD 20878
301-548-0150
www.iwla.org

KIDS FOR A CLEAN
ENVIRONMENT (KIDS
F.A.C.E.)
PO Box 158254
Nashville TN 32715
615-331-7381
www.kidsface.org

NATIONAL CLIMATIC DATA
CENTER
National Oceanic and Atmosphere
Administration
151 Patton Avenue
Asheville NC 28801
704-271-4800
www.noaa.gov

U.S. ENVIRONMENTAL
PROTECTION AGENCY
Public Information Reference Unit
401 M Street NW
Washington DC 20460
202-260-2090
www.epa.gov

U.S. FOREST SERVICE
PO Box 96090
Washington DC 20090
202-205-1760
www.fs.usda.gov

RAINFOREST ACTION
NETWORK
221 Pine Street
San Francisco CA 94104
415-398-4404
www.ran.org

SIERRA STUDENT COALITION
223 Thayer Street #2
Providence RI 02906
401-861-6012
www.ssc.org/ssc

SOLID WASTE INFORMATION
CLEARINGHOUSE
PO Box 7219

Silver Spring MD 20907
800-67-SWICH
www.swana.org

STUDENT ENVIRONMENTAL
ACTION COALITION
PO Box 31909
Philadelphia PA 19104
215-222-4711
www.seac.org

FAMILIES/PARENTING
(see also 1st - General; Child Abuse;
Education/Schools)

CHILDREN'S DEFENSE FUND
25 E Street NW
Washington DC 20001
202-628-8787
www.childrensdefense.org

CHILDREN'S RIGHTS
COUNCIL
300 Eye Street NE
Washington DC 20002
800-787-KIDS
www.vix.com/crc

CHILD WELFARE LEAGUE OF
AMERICA
440 First Street NW
Washington DC 20001
202-638-2952
www.cwla.org

COALITION FOR AMERICA'S
CHILDREN
1634 I Street
Washington DC 20006
202-638-5770
www.kidscampaign.org

FAMILY RESEARCH COUNCIL
801 G Street
Washington DC 20001
202-393-2100
www.frc.org

GENERATIONS UNITED
440 First Street NW #310
Washington DC 20001
202-662-4283
www.gu.org

JOSEPHSON INSTITUTE OF
ETHICS
Character Counts
4640 Admiralty Way
Manna del Ray CA 90292
310-306-1868
www.josephsoninstitute.org

NATIONAL ASSOCIATION OF
SOCIAL WORKERS
750 First Street NE
Washington DC 20002
202-408-8600
www.naswdc.org

NATIONAL CLEARINGHOUSE
ON FAMILIES AND YOUTH
PO Box 13505
Silver Spring MD 20911
301-608-8098
www.acf.dhhs.gov/ncfy

YOUTH!

NATIONAL COUNCIL ON
FAMILY RELATIONS
3989 Central Avenue NE
Columbia Heights MN 55421
612-781-9331
www.ncfr.com

NATIONAL FATHERHOOD
INITIATIVE
One Bank Street #160
Gaithersburg MD 20878
301-949-0599
www.register.com/father

TEEN PARENTING PROGRAMS
ERIC Clearinghouse on Urban
Education
Teachers College/Columbia University
Box 40
New York NY 10027
eric-web.tc.columbia.edu

HOMELESSNESS/
HUNGER

(see also Neighborhood Improvement;
Eating Disorders/Nutrition)

HABITAT FOR HUMANITY
INTERNATIONAL
121 Habitat Street
Americus GA 31709
800-422-4828
www.habitat.org

NATIONAL COALITION FOR
THE HOMELESS
1612 Connecticut Avenue NW
Washington DC 20006
202-265-2371 775 1322
nch.ari.net

NATIONAL RESOURCE
CENTER ON HOMELESSNESS
AND MENTAL ILLNESS
262 Delaware Avenue
Delmar NY 12054
800-444-7415
www.prainc.com/nrc

NATIONAL STUDENT
CAMPAIGN AGAINST
HUNGER AND
HOMELESSNESS
11965 Venice Blvd
Los Angeles CA 90066
800-No-Hunger
www.pirg.org/nscahh

U.S. DEPARTMENT OF
HOUSING AND URBAN
DEVELOPMENT
451 Seventh Street SW
Washington DC 20410
202-708-1420
www.hud.gov

TREVOR'S CAMPAIGN FOR
THE HOMELESS
3415 Westchester Pike
Newtown PA 19073
610-325-0640
www.youthventure.org/html/trevor_s

WHY (WORLD HUNGER
YEAR)
505 8th Avenue
New York NY 10018
800-5-HUNGRY
www.iglou.com/why

IMMIGRATION

(see also International; Constitutional
Rights; Discrimination/Racism)

FEDERATION FOR AMERICAN
IMMIGRATION REFORM
1666 Connecticut Avenue NW
Washington DC 20009
202-328-7004
www.fairus.org

NATIONAL COUNCIL OF
LA RAZA
810 First Street NE
Washington DC 20002
202-785-1670
www.nclr.com

NATIONAL IMMIGRATION
FORUM
220 Eye Street NE
Washington DC 20002
202-544-0004
www.immigrationforum.org

U.S. IMMIGRATION AND
NATURALIZATION SERVICE
425 Eye Street NW
Washington DC 20536
202-514-4316
www.ins.gov

INTERNATIONAL

(see also Environment; Immigration)

20/20 VISION
1828 Jefferson Place NW
Washington DC 20036
800-669-1782
vision@igc.apc.org

AMNESTY INTERNATIONAL
1118 22nd Street NW
Washington DC 20037
800-AMNESTY
www.amnesty.org

CENTER FOR DEFENSE
INFORMATION
1500 Massachusetts Avenue NW
Washington DC 20005
202-862-0700
galaxy.einet.net

FREE THE CHILDREN
INTERNATIONAL
12 East 48th Street
New York NY 10017
800-203-9091
www.freethechildren.org

FRIENDS OF THE EARTH
1025 Vermont Avenue NW
Washington DC 20005
202-783-7400
www.foe.org

GLOBAL YOUTH ACTION
NETWORK
211 N. 43rd St. #905
New York, NY 10017
212-661-6111
www.youthlink.org/gyan

UNITED NATIONS
United Nations Plaza
New York NY 10017
800-253-9646
www.un.org

WORLD RESOURCES
INSTITUTE
1735 New York Avenue NW
Washington DC 20006
202-638-6300
www.wri.org

WORLDWATCH INSTITUTE
1776 Massachusetts Ave NW
Washington DC 20036
202-452-1999
environlink.org

ZERO POPULATION GROWTH
1400 16th Street NW #320
Washington DC 20036
800-767-1956
www.zpg.org

INTERNET

(see also Constitutional Rights;
Education/Schools; TV/Movies;
Neighborhood Improvement)

CENTER FOR DEMOCRACY
AND TECHNOLOGY
1634 Eye Street NW
Washington DC 20006
202-637-9800
www.cdt.org

EDUCATION AND LIBRARY
NETWORK COALITION
c/o American Library Association
1301 Pennsylvania Avenue
Washington DC 20004
202-628-8421
www.itc.org/edlinc

KIDS SAFE
17939 Chatsworth Street #525
Grenado Hills CA 91344
800-320-9910
www.kidssafe.org

MIGHTY MEDIA INC.
400 First Avenue
Minneapolis MN 55401
800-644-4898
www.mightymedia.com

NATIONAL
TELECOMMUNICATIONS AND
INFORMATION
ADMINISTRATION
U.S. Department of Commerce
1401 Constitution Avenue
Washington DC 20230
202-482-5802
www.ntia.doc.gov

NEIGHBORHOOD IMPROVEMENT

(see also 1st—General; Community Service/Volunteerism; Crime/Violence Prevention; Education/Schools)

ALLIANCE FOR CIVIC RENEWAL
1445 Market Street
Denver CO 80208
303-571-4343
www.ncl.org/anr

BOYS & GIRLS CLUBS OF AMERICA
1230 W. Peachtree NW
Atlanta GA 30309
404-815-5804
www.bgca.org

NATIONAL 4-H COUNCIL
7100 Connecticut Avenue
Chevy Chase MD 20815
301-961-2800
www.fourhcouncil.edu

NATIONAL INSTITUTE ON OUT-OF-SCHOOL TIME
Center for Research on Women
Wellesley College
Wellesley MA 02181
617-283-2547
www.wellesley.edu/WCW/CRW/SAC

NATIONAL NEIGHBORHOOD COALITION
1875 Connecticut Avenue NW
Washington DC 20036
202-986-2539
www.comminforexch.org/nnc/html

PARTNERS FOR LIVABLE COMMUNITIES
1429 21st Street NW
Washington DC 20036
202-887-5990
www.livable.com

RESOURCES FOR YOUTH NEIGHBORHOOD MAPPING PROJECT
454 Las Gallinas Avenue
San Rafael CA 94903
415-331-5991
www.tcwf.org

YOUTH INITIATIVES
United Way of America
701 West Fairfax Street
Alexandria VA 22314
703-836-7100 ext 250
www.unitedway.org

YOUTH VENTURE
1700 North Moore Street
Arlington VA 22209
703-527-8300
www.youthventure.org

RELIGION

(see also Constitutional Rights; Discrimination/Racism; Education/Schools; Families/Parenting)

AMERICANS UNITED FOR SEPARATION OF CHURCH AND STATE
1816 Jefferson Place NW
Washington DC 20036
202-466-3234
www.au.org

CHRISTIAN COALITION
1801-L Sara Drive
Chesapeake VA 23320
757-424-2630
www.cc.org

INTERFAITH WORKING GROUP
PO Box 11706
Philadelphia PA 19101
215-235-3050
www.libertynet.org/iwg

NATIONAL CONFERENCE OF CHRISTIANS & JEWS
71 Fifth Avenue
New York NY 10003
800-352-6225

PEOPLE FOR THE AMERICAN WAY
2000 M Street NW
Washington DC 20036
800-326-PFAW
www.pfaw.org

RESPECTEEN
Lutheran Brotherhood
625 Fourth Avenue South
Minneapolis MN 55415
800-888-3820
www.luthbro.com

SEXUALITY

(see also 1st—General; Education/Schools; Families/Parenting; Religion)

ADVOCATES FOR YOUTH
1025 Vermont Avenue #200
Washington DC 20005
202-347-5700
www.advocatesforyouth.org

NATIONAL ABORTION AND REPRODUCTIVE RIGHTS ACTION LEAGUE
462 Broadway #540
New York NY 10013
212-343-0114
naralny@aol.com

NATIONAL ABSTINENCE ONLY CLEARINGHOUSE
801 E. 41st Street
Sioux Falls SD 57105
888-577-2966
www.abstinence.net

NATIONAL AIDS CLEARINGHOUSE
Centers for Disease Control
PO Box 6003
Rockville MD 20849
800-458-5231
www.cdc.gov

NATIONAL CAMPAIGN TO PREVENT TEEN PREGNANCY
1776 Massachusettes Ave.
Washington DC 20036
202-478-8524
www.teenpregnancy.org

NATIONAL ORGANIZATION ON ADOLESCENT PREGNANCY, PARENTING, PREVENTION
1319 F Street NW
Washington DC 20004
202-783-5770
www.noappp.org

NATIONAL RIGHT TO LIFE COMMITTEE
419 Seventh Street NW
Washington DC 20004
202-626-8800
www.nrlc.org

PLANNED PARENTHOOD FEDERATION OF AMERICA
810 Seventh Avenue
New York NY 10019
212-541-7800
www.plannedparenthood.org

SEXUALITY INFORMATION AND EDUCATION COUNCIL OF THE U.S.
130 W. 42nd Street #350
New York NY 10036
212-819-9770
www.siecus.org

SPORTS & EXERCISE

AMERICAN ALLIANCE OF HEALTH, PE, RECREATION & DANCE
1900 Association Drive
Reston VA 20191
703-476-3400
www.aahperd.org

NATIONAL ASSOCIATION FOR GIRLS AND WOMEN IN SPORTS
1900 Association Drive
Reston VA 22091
703-476-3452
www.aahperd.org

NATIONAL FEDERATION OF STATE HIGH SCHOOL ASSOCIATIONS
11724 NW Plaza Circle
Kansas City MO 64153
816-464-5400
www.nfhs.org

PRESIDENT'S COUNCIL ON PHYSICAL FITNESS AND SPORTS
450 Fifth Street NW
Washington DC 20001
202-272-2145
www.os.dhhs.gov/progorg/ophs/pcpfs

U.S. ASSOCIATION OF DISABLED ATHLETES
147 California Avenue
Uniondale NY 11553

YOUTH!

516-485-3701
www.wws.net/usoda

STUDENT LOANS
(see also Education/Schools)

AMERICAN ASSOCIATION OF
COMMUNITY COLLEGES
1 Dupont Circle
Washington DC 20036
202-728-0200
www.aacc.nche.edu

EDUCATIONAL RESOURCES
INFORMATION CENTER
(ERIC)
U.S. Department of Education
2277 Research Blvd
Rockville MD 20850
800-538-3742
www.aspensys.com/eric

FEDERAL STUDENT AID
INFORMATION
PO Box 84
Washington DC 20044
800-433-3243
www.ed.gov/offices/ope/students

NATIONAL ASSOCIATION OF
INDEPENDENT COLLEGES
AND UNIVERSITIES
1025 Connecticut Avenue NW
Washington DC 20036
202-785-8866
student-aid.nche.edu

U.S. STUDENT ASSOCIATION
1413 K Street NW
Washington DC 20005
202-347-8772
www.essential.org/ussa

SUICIDE/ DEPRESSION
*(see also 1st—General;
Education/Schools)*

AMERICAN FOUNDATION
FOR SUICIDE PREVENTION
120 Wall Street
New York NY 10005
212-410-1111
www.asfnet.org

MENTAL HEALTH PUBLIC
INQUIRIES
National Institute of Mental Health
5600 Fishers Lane Rm7C02
Rockville MD 20857
301-443-4513
www.nimh.nih.gov

SUICIDE AWARENESS VOICES
OF EDUCATION
PO Box 24507
Minneapolis MN 55424
612-946-7998
www.save.org

SUICIDE PREVENTION
ADVOCACY NETWORK
5034 Odin's Way
Marietta GA 30068
770-998-8819
www.spanusa.org

VIOLENCE PREVENTION
DIVISION
Centers of Disease Control
4770 Buford Highway MS-k60
Atlanta, GA 30341
770-488-4362
www.cdc.gov/ncipc

TOBACCO
*(see also Alcohol/Drugs;
Education/Schools)*

AMERICAN CANCER SOCIETY
1599 Clifton Road NE
Atlanta GA 30329
800-227-2345
www.acs.org

AMERICAN HEART
ASSOCIATION
7320 Greenville Avenue
Dallas TX 75231
800-242-8721
www.americanheart.org

AMERICAN LUNG
ASSOCIATION
1740 Broadway
New York NY 10019
800-LUNG-USA
www.lungusa.org

AMERICANS FOR
NONSMOKERS' RIGHTS
2530 San Pueblo Avenue
Berkeley CA 94702
510-841-3032
www.no-smoke.org

CAMPAIGN FOR TOBACCO-
FREE KIDS
1707 L Street NW
Washington DC 20036
800-284-KIDS
www.tobaccofreekids.org

DOCTORS OUGHT TO CARE
(DOC)
P.O. Box 20065
Seattle WA 98102
206-448-4946
www.kickbutt.org

NATIONAL SMOKERS
ALLIANCE
PO Box 1510
Merrifield VA 22116
703-739-1324
www.smokersalliance.org

OFFICE ON SMOKING AND
HEALTH
Centers for Disease Control
4770 Buford Highway NE MSK-50
Atlanta GA 30341
800-CDC-1311
www.cdc.gov/nccdphp/osh/tobacco.htm

SMOKEFREE EDUCATIONAL
SERVICES, INC.
PO Box 3316
New York NY 10008
212-912-0960
www.smokescreen.org/SES

STOP TEENAGE ADDICTION
TO TOBACCO
511 E. Columbus Avenue
Springfield MA 01105
413-732-7828
www.stat.org

TRUTH-AMERICAN LEGACY
FOUNDATION
1001 G Street, NW
Washington, D.C. 20001
202-454-5555
www.thetruth.com

TV/MOVIES
*(see also Advertising; Internet;
Families/Parenting; and pages 70-71)*

AMERICAN FAMILY
ASSOCIATION
107 Parkgate Drive #20D
Tupelo MS 38808
601-844-5036
www.afa.net

ASSOCIATION OF LOCAL
TELEVISION STATIONS
1320 19th Street
Washington DC 20036
202-887-1970
www.altv.com

CITIZENS FOR MEDIA
LITERACY
34 Wall Street
Asheville NC 28801
704-255-0182
www.main.nc.us/cml

ENVIRONMENT MEDIA
ASSOCIATION
3679 Motor Avenue
Los Angeles CA 90034
310-287-2803
www.epg.org

FEDERAL COMMUNICATIONS
COMMISSION
Mass Media Bureau
1919 M Street NW
Washington DC 20554
202-632-6860
www.fcc.gov

JUSTTHINK
221 Caledonia Street
Sausalito CA 94965
415-289-0122
www.justthink.org

KIDSNET
6846 Eastern Avenue
Washington DC 20012
202-291-1400
www.familyeducation.com

MEDIASCOPE
12711 Ventura Blvd
Studio City CA 91604
818-508-2080
www.mediascope.org

MOTION PICTURE
ASSOCIATION
1600 Eye Street NW
Washington DC 20036
202-293-1966
www.mppa.org

C H A P T E R 3
It's Your Freedom,
It's Your Right

The First Amendment

> "Congress shall make no law ... abridging
> the freedom of speech, or of the press, or the
> right of the people peaceably to assemble,
> and to petition the Government
> for a redress of grievances."
> —The Bill of Rights

Just like playing any sport, trying different tactics to make your point is essential. A surprise move or ambush against the other side often can work to your favor. Other times, a more cautious approach may be just as successful. The range of strategies covered in this chapter, many of which demand practice and commitment, can help your team's game plan succeed. Stay confident and remember that it's your right to speak up for what you believe in. Don't let anyone interfere with that!

DEMOCRACY FOR UNDER $1

For the price of a piece of paper, an envelope, and a stamp, you can make your position known. Don't ever doubt that every letter counts.

A state legislator once announced on the chamber floor that he "got so much mail in support of that bill!" that he had to vote for it. How many letters did this Utah senator actually receive? Six. Remember this true story when you wonder whether it's worth writing a letter to register your views to members of your school board, perhaps the mayor, or a corporate executive. Short letters that contain strong convictions and solid information continue to rank as an easy, effective and cheap way to communicate with the powers-that-be. Thanks to fax machines and e-mail, your opinions and pleas for action can be sent instantly without spending any money on postage.

In your letter, be brief and to-the-point. Avoid form letters because they may not get read. (Personal notes that reveal your genuine concern will get noticed.) Sometimes, a legible handwritten letter may actually get more attention; it looks a lot more authentic and heartfelt than a computer-generated one. Also, **state clearly what you would like done** and, in cases of legislation, mention the specific bill by number or title. If you should decide on a letter-writing blitz where people sign pre-printed postcards or letters, try to deliver them in person and alert the news media the day before.

Since elected officials and prominent community leaders respond to public pressure, another tactic is to recycle your letter into a public statement by changing the heading from "Dear Governor" to "Open Letter to the Governor" or to whomever your audience is. Then submit this article to the **daily newspaper** or fax it to radio and TV stations. If you succeed in interesting the media in your issue, reporters may seek a quote from the decision-maker. This spotlight can get powerful people to respond publicly to your demands.

Because of the volume of mail some decision-makers receive, it is rare that you will get back a personal letter from either the decision-maker or a member of his/her staff. In fact, your letter may not get a reply at all or you may only get a form letter in return, thanking you for your interest and concern. **If you aren't satisfied with the response you get, don't give up.** Write again and make sure to mention that the response you received was confusing or vague. Ask the decision-maker to clarify his/her position. Your second letter is much more likely to get the attention and respect it deserves.

FROM A LETTER TO PUBLIC BILLBOARD

A girl concerned about the level of ozone depletion wrote to George Bush, U.S. President at the time. Disappointed by the form letter she received from the White House, Melissa Poe got a local advertising company to agree to blow up her handwritten letter on a huge billboard for only $50.00. She raised the money by selling lemonade and plums and holding a yard sale.

Dear Mr. President,
Please will you do something about pollution. I want to live till I am 100 years old.
Mr. President, if you ignore this letter we will all die of pollution.
Please Help!
Melissa Poe, Age 9
Nashville, Tennessee

This public plea led Melissa to start Kids For A Clean Environment, better known as Kids F.A.C.E., which now has hundreds of chapters nationwide.

Tips When sending a letter to a lawmaker, use your campaign letterhead with your mailing address and phone number so the decision-maker can reply to you.

Include the full name and address of the person to whom you are writing. Be respectful and use formal titles. For many elected officials, the first line of the address should read "The Honorable" followed by his/her name and position.

Use a colon instead of a comma after the "Dear" section.

Identify yourself by name and explain who you are. Be personal. Some young people prefer not to mention their age because they want their ideas to be judged on merit only; others believe that disclosing their age can benefit their cause.

105 River's End
Seaford, DE 19973

January 5, 1997

The Honorable Michael
United States House of
Washington, D.C. 20515

Formal salutation

ar Representative Castle:

Identify yourself

the past few years, state and federal governments have
been unable to decide at what age an American is legally an
adult.   In Delaware I can drive a car at sixteen.   At
eighteen, I can vote for a president of the United States
and go to war to fight and die for my country. Not until I'm
twenty-one can I legally drink a beer. The legal system
confuses the matter even further.   I am subject to
punishment as an adult at eighteen, unless it is a really
bad crime, when the age of adulthood is deemed sixteen.

Stick to one issue

The inconsistencies in these age limits are illogical. My
government thinks I'm responsible enough to drive a two ton
car at sixty miles an hour at the age of sixteen, but not
old enough to make a responsible choice of who I want to
lead my country. My government says that if I am eighteen
years of age, I can walk through an East Asian jungle with
M16 killing people, but I can't walk through my living
room with a margarita.

Use facts to make your case

I believe it's time we decide at what age a citizen becomes
an adult and the privileges of drinking, voting, and driving
should go with the responsibility of fighting for one's
country and being held legally responsible for one's
actions.

I would like you to introduce legislation that would d
the legal age eighteen for becoming an adult.   I beli
states should raise the driving age and lower the drinking
age to be consistent with the current legal voting age. Al
rights, privileges, and responsibilities should be given at
the same time, a person's eighteenth birthday. If I can help
by sending more letters I would be glad to do so.

Be clear what you want changed

Sincerely,

Ry Culver

Demonstrate your commitment

Stick to one issue per letter. Be clear and concise so you don't confuse the person who
is reading your letter. Also, keep your letter short, usually one page.

Use facts to support your position. Whenever possible, include personal knowledge,
an anecdote, or some other information to be more persuasive. Explain what kind of
action or response you would like the decision-maker to consider, for example,
meeting with your group, voting for or against a particular proposal, or for the
decision-maker to ask his or her colleagues to support your initiative as well (you
might suggest that he/she write a "Dear Colleague" letter).

Demonstrate your determination and ongoing commitment. Ry Culver writes in the
final sentence of his letter to his congressman, "If I can help by sending more letters I
would be glad to do so."

LETTERS TO THE EDITOR

Students deserve a fair hearing before suspension

■ Students deserve a fair hearing before they are suspended from school. Currently, West Hartford students are suspended immediately after a "dangerous weapon" is found [news story, Nov. 3, "Schools taking a stand. Do 'zero tolerance' policies go too far?"].

When a student is found with a "dangerous weapon," the following procedure is followed by the administration to inform the student of the offense.

- You have been caught with a knife.
- You will be suspended for at least five days.
- The student is then asked if he or she has anything to say. No matter what the student says, the principal issues a five-plus-day suspension.

We _____ problem with this. In this country, student _____ _____ so that the safety of the school _____ _____ _____ of the individual. We agree that sch_____ _____ _____ and we want our schools to continue _____ _____ _____ not whether students can carry weap_____ _____. We should agree with a common-sense weap_____ policy. A student must know that he or she cannot bring a weapon into school. There should be consequences for students who bring weapons into school.

However, students should receive an oral or written warning of the charges. If the student denies the charges, an explanation can be given and the student may give his or her side of the story.

What's the point of letting a student respond when a punishment has already been determined? The fact that there is no appeals process is not right. This puts any student's future in the hands of an administrator who must make a decision about a suspension quickly.

West Hartford recently amended its suspension policy by imposing a new five-day minimum suspension instead of the former 10-day minimum.

According to the new policy, administrators are able to use discretion when they choose the penalty for a student who brings a weapon into school.

This change is only a baby step in the right direction. We believe an appeals board needs to be _____ to decide on the length of the suspension. _____ _____ _____ would consist of students, parents, _____ _____ _____ _____ counselors and administrators. _____ _____ _____ _____ _____ _____ the "minimum Guideline _____ _____ _____ _____ _____ _____ sentence" should b_____ _____ _____ _____ _____ story of

A student with a clean re_____ _____ minimum behavioral problems should receive a _____ _____ sentence for bringing a Swiss Army knife or other small dangerous instrument to school if it is not used in a dangerous manner and if there is no mali_____ cious intent. A student with a record of fights and/or behavioral problems should be given a harsher sentence.

Bea Smilowitz
West Hartford

Editor's note: The writer is sophomore class president a_____ Hall High School in West Hartford and chairman of th_____ International Student Activism Alliance. The letter wa_____ signed also by four other alliance members.

NEWSPAPER ARTICLE SPARKS DEBATE

PICK UP THE PHONE

The telephone remains a powerful connection. Elected officials in Columbia, South Carolina, got an earful after the City Council reneged on its promise to provide funding for the salary of a staff director at a local teen center. Student organizers developed a telephone tree and got their friends and parents to call council members at their homes. The concerted effort paid off: the money for the center was restored.

*(For more information, see **Telephone Tips** in Chapter 1: Doing the Detective Work.)*

26% *at work*

SIGN HERE, PLEASE!

Petitions are another inexpensive way to let decision-makers know how you and many others feel about a particular issue. Dozens or hundreds of signatures can be a real wake-up call for politicians and business leaders who have shut their eyes and turned their backs on the problem. Presenting stacks of signed petitions in a public forum can be effective and put pressure on officials to take notice, especially with reporters there and TV cameras rolling. In addition, the process of collecting signatures gets the word out and can boost your recruitment efforts. You may even meet a few signers who want to join your campaign!

Here are a few petition pointers:

LOOK OFFICIAL. Use your letterhead and logo or identify your organization as the sponsor. Include the address and phone number of your group so supporters can return completed petitions or get in contact with you for more information.

BE CLEAR. State the purpose of the petition—for example, to support or oppose a school-based HIV testing site. If your petition is in response to a proposed ordinance or bill, state the name and number of the proposal and a brief summary of its provisions.

PLEDGE CARDS:
A Compelling Alternative to Petitions

Politicians may disregard petitions if they think the demands listed do not reflect the views of their constituents. Signing a petition requires little thought or commitment. Some people scribble their name on a petition because it's easier than saying no. A pledge card can have a bit more bite. Pledge cards simply state that a person supports an issue so much that they will promise to do something if action is not taken by the decision-maker. A person could refuse to vote for the politician, refrain from buying a certain product from a company, or refuse to make donations to an organization. Besides the individual commitment, a stack of several hundred pledge cards looks much more impressive than five or six pieces of paper with an equal number of signatures.

STATE YOUR REASONS. Describe briefly the arguments for your position by including a few facts. This information will add credibility to your petition and may convince some people who would not otherwise consider signing to lend their name in support of your initiative.

ALLOW ENOUGH SPACE. Design a petition with enough space for each person to print and sign his or her name and address. Consider a column for phone numbers and possibly e-mail addresses, so you can contact people in the future. You may also want to have a space for age and/or grade if the petition addresses a school issue. If a petition is directed to an elected official, include the signer's complete address and perhaps voting district.

SET A DATE. Consider including on all petitions a deadline and any other instructions that may be important.

When you have designed your petition, all you have left to do is get signatures. Since some people don't want to be the first to sign their name, suggest to everybody helping that they sign their name (only once) on the blank petition they intend to circulate. Then find a busy sidewalk or street corner or set up a table outside of your supermarket. You can even circulate your petition at school and have friends at other schools collect signatures. A word of caution: get permission first if you will be collecting signatures on private property. That might include the area just outside of the grocery store. It's your right to petition, but your right ends when it infringes upon the rights of others. For instance, if you pass your petition around school, do it before or after class or during lunch. Also, never pressure anyone into signing a petition. Think about keeping a tally of signatures collected and when the number is impressive, tell the news media.

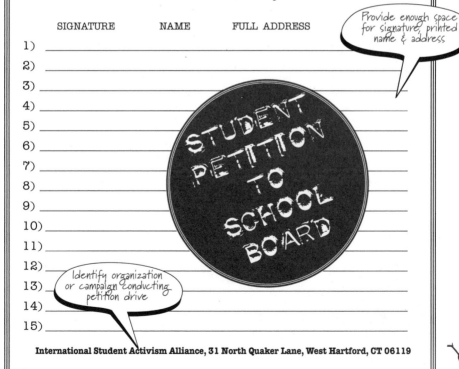

To Dr. Sklarz and Board of Education members:

State your purpose & reasons

We are very upset with the decision regarding the extension of the high school day by 10 minutes at the beginning of the school day for the 1996-97 school year. We believe that the school day begins too early as it is. We require sleep in order to function properly in all of our classes. According to this new proposal, those of us who travel by bus to school will be leaving our homes in the winter months while it is still dark. We understand that the school day needs to be lengthened, but due to our concern for our safety, well being, and education, the beginning of the school day is not an appropriate place to add on minutes. Instead, we suggest that the minutes be added to the end of the school day or another time that will not interfere with our ability to focus in class.

	SIGNATURE	NAME	FULL ADDRESS

Provide enough space for signature, printed name & address

1)
2)
3)
4)
5)
6)
7)
8)
9)
10)
11)
12)
13)
14)
15)

Identify organization or campaign conducting petition drive

STUDENT PETITION TO SCHOOL BOARD

International Student Activism Alliance, 31 North Quaker Lane, West Hartford, CT 06119

MAKING NEWS:
SPREADING THE WORD

A little publicity goes a long way. A letter to the editor, a passing comment made by the DJ over the airwaves, a 90-second story on the evening news, or an article in the weekly newspaper can mean instant credibility and prompt other journalists to jump on the bandwagon and write stories. Students you don't know from faraway schools, organizations you've never heard of, and complete strangers from other states will hear about your efforts and some will want to join in. Your network of contacts will multiply and diversify. In

CREATING A POWERFUL "SOUND BITE"

Reporters and decision-makers often tune out when they hear the same statistics and familiar slogans like "Just Say No" over and over again. A fresh, hard-hitting message can capture their attention and make them remember you and your campaign. This 20-second "sound bite" has a good chance of getting broadcast on the evening news or being the quote that appears in newspaper articles. Here are a few examples of effective quotes that young activists have invented. They have been used in letters to elected officials, newspaper editorials, a public service announcement, and at a news conference.

"WHY CAN A KID GET A GUN IN A FEW HOURS, BUT HAVE TO TAKE A BUS OUTSIDE THE NEIGHBORHOOD TO BUY SCHOOL SUPPLIES?" —Sherman Spears with Teens on Target at a news conference in Oakland, California, urging passage of a local law that would make guns less available.

"THE NEIGHBORS ADJACENT TO OUR SCHOOL ARE GROWING A DUMP INSTEAD OF FLOWERS." —A letter written by a group of students in Springfield, Massachusetts, to their city council member who responded immediately by getting the mountain of addition, the people you are trying to influence will digest just about every tidbit and feel the pressure to do something. This media spotlight can cause decision-makers to become more responsive to your campaign.

The chief challenge is competing for headlines. Your initiative needs to be presented as interesting and fresh, preferably with a hint of **controversy**. As they say in the newsroom, "If it's not new, it's not news." But you have an advantage. It is not all that common for ordinary citizens, especially young people, to speak out and take the lead in tackling today's problems. The news media adores this human interest angle.

dangerous trash hauled away. (The school's principal had tried for three years to get the city to clear the dump site.)

"TO PEE OR NOT TO PEE, THAT IS THE QUESTION." —Headline of a Maryland high school newspaper editorial that led to a county-wide, student-run news conference on locked bathrooms and other policies that fail to enforce the no-tobacco use law on school property.

"THESE ARE ORDINARY PEOPLE. ORDINARY PEOPLE WITH HIV...IF YOU DON'T THINK YOU NEED HIV EDUCATION, WE'VE SAVED A SPACE FOR YOU," FOLLOWED BY THE AIDS HOTLINE. —High school students in Portland, Maine, produced this award-winning 30-second public service announcement that was broadcast on Fox TV.

"AS A PEER EDUCATOR, I KNOW THAT MY FRIENDS AND OTHER STUDENTS DEPEND ON OUR FAMILY LIFE CURRICULUM. IF YOU KILL HEALTH ED, MORE TEENAGERS ARE GOING TO BE KILLED BY DRUGS, DRUNK DRIVING AND AIDS. WE NEED MORE THAN 5¢ PER STUDENT. AREN'T OUR LIVES WORTH MORE THAN A STICK OF GUM!" —A New York high school student from Buffalo speaking out against proposed school health education budget cuts.

CREATING A POWERFUL "SOUND BITE"

Usually when you call, you will want to speak to the assignment editor at the different radio or TV stations and a particular reporter or the managing editor of both daily and weekly newspapers. Before calling these busy people, it's good to **develop a short sales pitch and practice it** with a friend. In addition to giving details about a petition drive, an upcoming summit or some other event, include a punch line that highlights the importance of what you are trying to do. This compelling **"sound bite"** can be reused many times in a news release, a speech, or during an interview with a reporter.

It would be ideal if your media contacts include a variety of print, radio, and TV journalists. To get names and addresses, you can rely on people you know at well-established community organizations that have communications or public relations offices. Another approach is to build your own media list, using resources such as *Gale's Directory of Publications and Broadcast Media* that can be found at the reference desk of your public library. This easy-to-use source identifies all newspapers, radio and television stations in every city and town. Because news directors and editors change frequently, call to check whether the information is still correct. Also inquire about which reporter covers education, crime, or whatever "beat" that corresponds to the issue you're concerned about. Confirm the spelling of that person's full name and fax number so you can fax your news release to save time and avoid the cost of postage.

In addition, make sure to identify statewide contacts, especially the **Associated Press (AP)** *wire service that has at least one news bureau in each state, usually located in the state capital. If you can interest an AP reporter to file a story, bingo! The story will be sent "over the wire" to just about every news media outlet in the entire state. Newspapers might run the article, and TV stations could pick up the story and do a feature on your campaign. Newsworthy or unusual AP stories get sent to the national wire service and wind up being reported on* **CNN, MTV**, *and other networks.*

(The addresses and phone numbers for a handful of national media outlets are listed in INFO-STARTERS on pages 70-71.)

YOUTH!

When you finally get a chance to talk to a reporter, don't be surprised if you are asked simple, open-ended questions. One reason is that reporters usually don't know much about specific issues. So expect questions like "What do your friends think about what you are trying to do?" or "How did you get involved?" These non-threatening questions are fine, but they take away **precious time** from the main message you want to get across. Try to avoid telling long stories of how you got involved or what your friends and family think. Instead, move to the major point you want to make: give them a quotable quote and use your "sound bite." Another effective tactic is to answer a question briefly and then make another point without waiting for the next question.

RESPONDING TO A REPORTER'S "GOTCHA" QUESTIONS

Be aware that controversy is a crucial aspect of any story. Rather than focusing on the issue itself, sometimes reporters will ask why you are allowed to miss school, unlike your classmates. Reporters may test your knowledge and throw some curve balls your way. For example, if you are pushing for drug treatment services you may get asked about the legalization of marijuana. A casual answer could end up being on the evening news or in the morning newspaper, instead of the key issues you raised about drug rehab. Be ready for these "gotcha" questions and try to avoid getting trapped. One strategy is to answer by saying that this is not an issue you've studied and immediately return to your hard-hitting message. Don't worry if you're repeating yourself because picking out key quotes for an article or TV story is the editor's job!

NEWS RELEASES IN 500 WORDS OR LESS

A news release, often called a press release or news advisory, is simply a one- or two-page statement that describes an event or makes an annnouncement. It's usually sent by snail mail, e-mail, or fax to individual news media outlets and community leaders to increase interest in an issue or to request their attendance at a news conference, rally or some other activity.

REMEMBER TO ADDRESS THE "FIVE W'S":

 WHY—Let people know why you are taking action. Your reason may strike a nerve with others and motivate them to get involved, too.

 WHAT—Describe what is unique, important, and newsworthy about your campaign or this event.

WHERE—Be sure to let reporters and photographers know where the event is being held. Consider a well-known location that will offer good visuals for the cameras.

WHEN—Morning, noon, or evening? To make the evening news, an event should be held before 4 p.m. Also, Mondays and Fridays tend to be slower news days and reporters often have to hunt for stories to cover. If you have a rally on a weekend, then you will not have to compete with as many other stories, but there will usually be fewer camera crews and reporters working. Weigh your options carefully.

WHO—Mention the student group, youth organization, or alliance involved and include a quote ("sound bite") by at least one of the student leaders and perhaps a well-known adult supporter. A bit of background information about your group or campaign can help to get more serious attention from the press corps.

Also, list the name, address, and phone number of your group's contact person, so that reporters know whom to contact for more information. The rest is up to you. Take a look at the example on the next page for a few additional suggestions.

Two weeks before a scheduled event, mail or fax your news release to your media contacts. Hand-delivering your news release can also be very effective. Then call to check if they got your information. Press releases arrive by the hundreds and often get lost or misplaced, so expect to have to send out another copy. On the morning of the event, call each newspaper and radio and TV stations to make your sales pitch once more and remind them of the time and place.

Use official stationery or letterhead with your campaign's or organization's name.

1

S T U D E N T   A L L I A N C E

SA

220 South State Street
Chicago, Illinois 60604-2101
Phone: 312/922-5150 Fax: 312/922-4193
e-mail: info@studentalliance.org

1

For Immediate Release
Wednesday, June 14, 1995
<u>Contact</u>: Phillip Bleicher,
Executive Director 312-922-5150

2

3

Create a headline that will stand out from the dozens of other news releases.

Students Demand Meeting with "Education Mayor"

5,000 Letters to be Presented for Students' Super Board Proposal

[Chicago, IL] — *Chicago Public School students will gather on the 5th floor of CITY HALL, 121 North LaSalle Street, THURSDAY, JUNE 15 at 10:00AM.   Student leaders will present over 5,000 letters collected* **4** *past two weeks requesting Mayor Daley to appoint a student to the new "Super Board."*

Make sure to answer the questions: why, what, where, when, who.

"Students have been shut-out of school reform, and this is an opportunity for the consumers, in other words students, to participate," said Jerome Bailey, Chicago Board of Education Student Member and junior at King High School.

Use a strong quote.

5

"We are confident that the 'Education Mayor' would not refuse a meeting with us the same way he would not deny a meeting with business leaders," adds 17-year-old Roberto Silva, President of the Chicago Local School Council Student M *rs and student at Wells High School.*

6

Another "sound bite."

The Student Alliance believes a high school student with full voting power on the "Super Board" represents the student body on issues that affect them most. Such student representation currently exists in other U.S. cities; therefore, the Stude *nce is seeking equality for Chicago students.*

7

If space permits, include additional background information to add legitimacy to your group or event.

Student leaders attending will be: Nathaniel Branscomb, President of Student Alliance and Hyde Park Career Academy junior; Vanessa Perez, Student Alliance Vice-President and Prosser High School LSC Student Member; Goran Davidovac, Taft High School LSC Student Member; Roberto Silva, President of the Chicago LSC Student Members and Wells High School LSC Student Member; Jerome Bailey, Chicago Board of Education Student Member and King High School student; and Phillip Bleicher, Executive Director of Student Alliance and former student member of the Chicago Board of Education.

\#

8

List the name, address, phone and/or pager number of a contact person (someone who can receive and return calls between 10 am - 5 pm).

At the end of the news release, near the bottom of the page, write "#" or "- 30 -" to signify the end.

PRESS CONFERENCES...
LIGHTS! CAMERAS! ACTION!!!

A press conference can be a superb publicity move, similar to holding a rally but involving fewer people. Like a march or demonstration, however, a tremendous amount of effort, creativity, and skill is required—even though a press conference usually lasts less than an hour, including time for short speeches and questions.

If your news is truly newsworthy, a press conference will capture the media's attention and raise public awareness of your campaign. If not, your time may be better spent working on the other details of your game plan. After all, why plan something to which no one will come? A news release may be a smarter strategy now. Members of the press can always be invited to a meeting or event later on. In any case, definitely get some advice and media contacts from your adult allies and others who are experienced in staging press conferences. Their help can save you a lot of time and trouble in the process.

IF YOU DO DECIDE TO CONDUCT A PRESS CONFERENCE, HERE ARE A FEW TIPS:

LOCATION: Hold the event in a convenient place for the media, such as town hall or the state capitol. Usually reporters will not travel great distances to cover a press conference.

ROOM SIZE: Avoid a huge auditorium and opt for a small room that will not look empty. Remember, a breaking story across town can mean a disappointing turnout, but making follow-up calls to reporters can still mean capturing air time or space in the local newspaper.

SPEAKERS: Choose your speakers carefully. Each one should address a different aspect of the issue. Take into consideration your goal, purpose, mood, location, and your audience.

VISUAL PROPS: As always, include visuals in your presentation. Cameras need footage other than "talking heads." Create banners and posters showcasing your group's name along with graphs or blown-up photographs to make your campaign that much more real.

PUBLICIZE: Send out news releases far enough in advance to alert the media. You may want to divide up your media list and assign different people to get on the phone with reporters and assignment editors. Plan to call each media contact several times, including a final reminder on the day of your press conference.

VIPs: Invite community leaders and potential supporters to the press conference. If a public official supports your campaign, you can also ask him or her to speak, but set a time limit. Prominent figures can attract journalists who would not normally consider attending.

PRESS PACKETS: Prepare information packets for everyone who attends and include such items as a copy of the news release, fact sheets on the issue, and short biographies of each speaker. Make sure that every statistic is checked for accuracy and all materials are carefully "proofed" for typos and errors.

PRACTICE: At the dress rehearsal, use a video camera or tape recorder. Practice your "sound bite" so this punch line rolls off your tongue with ease. You can also use a role-play situation, responding to possible questions you might be asked by reporters, in order to rehearse.

STAGE FRIGHT: When speaking, be aware of your breathing, gestures, posture, facial expressions, voice, and eye contact. It's normal to be nervous. Calm down and do your best. Speak from your heart and your head.

STEPPING UP TO THE MICROPHONE

STATEMENT BY JANELLE OLLIVIERRE
UNPLUG/UNIVERSITY OF MASS-AMHERST PRESS CONFERENCE
NATIONAL PRESS CLUB, FIRST AMENDMENT ROOM
12 NOON
WASHINGTON, D.C.
TUESDAY, OCTOBER 19th, 1993

MY NAME IS JANELLE OLLIVIERRE AND I AM A JUNIOR AT CALVIN COOLIDGE SENIOR HIGH SCHOOL HERE IN WASHINGTON D.C. I HOPE TO FINISH COLLEGE ONE DAY AND BECOME A TEACHER AND EVENTUALLY OWN AND RUN MY OWN DAYCARE CENTERS.

I AM HERE TODAY BECAUSE I DISAGREE WITH CHANNEL ONE BEING IN MY SCHOOL FOR MANY REASONS. I FEEL, FIRST OF ALL, THAT IF SOMEBODY WANTS TO GIVE URBAN SCHOOLS MONEY OR PRODUCTS, THEY SHOULD GIVE BASIC THINGS WE NEED LIKE BETTER BOOKS AND DESKS AND MORE COMPUTERS.

I ALSO THINK THAT CHANNEL ONE TAKES UP TOO MUCH CLASS TIME. YOU HAVE TO STOP WHATEVER YOU'RE LEARNING, NO MATTER HOW IMPORTANT IT IS, AND WATCH THE TV BECAUSE IT COMES ON AUTOMATICALLY. THE ONLY THING YOU CAN DO IS UNPLUG THE TV SINCE WE HAVE NO CONTROL OVER THE ON/OFF BUTTON.

THE WORST THING ABOUT CHANNEL ONE IS THAT IT'S BORING. MOST OF MY FRIENDS TRY TO IGNORE IT. IT DOESN'T DEAL WITH URBAN SCHOOLS OR STUDENTS EVEN THOUGH IT'S SHOWN IN URBAN SCHOOLS AND TO URBAN STUDENTS.

IN CLOSING, I WOULD LIKE TO SAY THAT I THINK EDUCATION IS VERY, VERY IMPORTANT, BUT CHANNEL ONE ISN'T NECESSARY BECAUSE IT DOESN'T DO ITS JOB. IT DOESN'T EDUCATE.

YOUTH!

Make sure to **publicize your efforts beyond your own school audience** (student newspaper, school radio station or television news program, etc.) in order to reach key community leaders and decision-makers. Besides sending out an eye-catching news release or staging some event, participate in **radio talk shows** either as a caller or as a guest. Contact local stations or the community cable access channel with ideas such as producing a documentary, a special, or a 30-second public service announcement. Approach an advertising company to donate a billboard for your message or for help in raising money for a paid advertisement. You should continually evaluate how your proposal is presented and whether it can be tied to other issues that are currently in the news. Never distort or exaggerate because the news media will not give you the time of day if they have reason to believe you are not being completely truthful.

DONUTS TO DJs = AIR TIME

High school students campaigning to remove drunk drivers from the road wanted a big crowd at their rally. In pairs, students visited dozens of radio stations with their news release and some donuts. This friendly gesture got them into the studios to talk LIVE about their event during the busy morning rush hour.

As you will undoubtedly find, the trick to winning media attention is to experiment with lots of publicity strategies. If you fail to get any bites the first time, try again. **Be clever**. Unusual stunts get noticed and will be remembered far longer than what has been read in a newspaper or heard over the airwaves. A personal favorite of ours is "Toilet Talk:" a group that advertised in public restrooms. They placed posters on the walls in front of urinals and on the doors of stalls, and even wrote messages on the sheets of the rolls of toilet paper. Remember, don't keep it a secret. Publicize!

NEWS MEDIA

I't's always best to send your news release to an individual. When you call to verify the mailing addresses below, be sure to ask for the names of editors or producers who might be interested in your story. Then send your release specifically to them, possibly along with a brief, hand-written note. If no e-mail address or fax number is listed, the national media organization prefers to receive information by mail.

ABC TELEVISION NETWORK
77 W. 66th Street
New York NY 10023-6201
212-456-7777 News Fax: 212-456-2795
e-mail: abc@aol.com

AMERICAN NEWS SERVICE
Center for Living Democracy
RR1 Black Fox Road
Brattleboro VT 05301
800-654-NEWS Fax: 802-254-1227
e-mail: ebernheim@americannews.com
www.americannews.com

ASSOCIATED PRESS (AP) WIRE SERVICE
2021 K Street NW #600
Washington DC 20006
202-776-9400 Fax: 202-776-9570
www.wireap.org

ASSOCIATED PRESS (AP) BROADCAST NEWS
1825 K Street NW #710
Washington DC 20500
800-821-4747 News Fax: 202-736-1199

BLUE JEAN Magazine
7353 Pittsford-Victor Road #201
Victor NY 14564
716-924-4080
e-mail: editors@bluejeans.org
www.bluejeanmag.com

CBS TELEVISION NETWORK
524 W. 57th Street
New York NY 10019-2902
212-975-4114 News Fax: 212-975-1893
e-mail: realitycheck@cbsnews.com

CHANNEL ONE TV
5300 Melrose Avenue/4th Floor
Los Angeles CA 90038
213-860-1200 News Fax: 213-860-1450
www.channelone.com

CHILDREN'S EXPRESS Newspaper
1331 H Street #900
Washington DC 20005
202-737-7377 Fax: 202-737-0193
www.ce.org

CNN/CABLE NEWS NETWORK
PO Box 105366
Atlanta GA 30348
404-827-1511 News Fax: 404-681-3578
www.cnn.com

FOX BROADCASTING COMPANY
10201 W Pico Blvd
Los Angeles CA 90064-2606
310-369-1000 Fax: 310-369-1433
e-mail: foxnet@delphi.com

IN THE MIX/PBS TV
102 E. 30th Street
New York NY 10016-7369
212-684-3940 Fax: 212-684-4015
e-mail: inthemix@aol.com

MTV/MUSIC TELEVISION
1515 Broadway 23rd Floor
New York NY 10036-8901
212-258-8736 Fax: 212-258-8844
www.mtv.com/news

NATIONAL PUBLIC RADIO (NPR)
625 Massachusetts Avenue NW
Washington, DC 20001
202-414-2000 Fax: 202-414-3329
e-mail: "Morning Edition" morning@npr.org
e-mail: "All Things Considered" atc@npr.org
e-mail: "Talk of the Nation" totn@npr.org
www.npr.org

NBC TELEVISION NETWORK
30 Rockefeller Plaza
New York NY 10112-0002
212-664-4691 News Fax: 212-583-5453
e-mail: nbc@aol.com

NEWSWEEK
251 West 57th Street
New York NY 10019
212-445-4000 Fax: 212-445-5068
www.newsweek.com

NICK NEWS/NICKELODEON
96 Morton Street
New York NY 10014-3326
212-463-0029 News Fax: 212-463-7049

YOUTH!

OPRAH WINFREY SHOW
Harpo Productions
110 North Carpenter
Chicago IL 60607
Fax: 312-633-1976
e-mail: oprah@aol.com

PBS/PUBLIC BROADCASTING SERVICE
1320 Braddock Place
Alexandria VA 22314-1649
703-739-5000 Fax: 703-739-5295
e-mail: viewer@pbs.org

PEOPLE Magazine
1271 Sixth Avenue
New York NY 10020
212-522-1212 Fax: 212-522-0331
www.people.com

PUBLIC RADIO INTERNATIONAL (PRI)
100 N. 6th Street #900A
Minneapolis MN 55403
612-338-5000 Fax: 612-330-9222
www.pri.org

USA TODAY
1000 Wilson Blvd
Arlington VA 22229
703-276-6536
www.usatoday.com

US NEWS & WORLD REPORT
2400 N Street NW
Washington DC 20037
202-955-2000 Fax: 202-955-2049
www.usnews.com

SCHOLASTIC UPDATE Magazine
555 Broadway
New York NY 10012
212-343-6271 Fax: 212-343-6619
www.scholastic.com

TEEN PEOPLE Magazine
1271 Sixth Avenue
New York NY 10020
212-522-2179 Fax: 212-467-4633
e-mail: teenpeople@aol.com

TIME Magazine
Rockefeller Center
New York NY 10020
212-522-1212 Fax: 212-522-2815
www.time.com

WHO CARES Magazine
1511 K Street NW
Washington DC 20005
202-628-1691 Fax: 202-628-2063
e-mail: info@whocares.org
www.whocares.org

FACE-TIME AND PRESENTATION POINTERS

Yes, face-time! It's slang for being seen and seeing others. In a campaign, chance meetings or scheduled appointments with people in powerful positions can really make things happen. There is no substitute for personal contact.

You might start thinking about people you know and the people they know. Explore your connections. For instance, your mother might work with a member of the school board. The son of a state senator could be a student in your class. These relationships can make it easier for you to gain access to the ears and opinions of key decision-makers. High-powered people may also be more willing to listen because they know you indirectly. However, don't hesitate for even a second if you don't know someone, or know someone who knows someone. You're not automatically out of the loop. **After all, it's what you know that really counts!**

> "Know your leaders, your city officials. Write down your concerns. Have meetings and put together a list of things you'd like to see happen. The worst they can say is no, but you can keep trying."
> — Augusto Rodriguez, High school student and Young Adult Police Commissioner, New Haven, CT

If your connections, or lack of connections, fail to produce a meeting, consider the traditional approach for getting a face-to-face session with an important official: calling to get an appointment. You may have to call repeatedly or you can opt to make a written request to schedule a date. **Writing** also enables you to enclose information such as your mission statement or survey results so that these community heavyweights recognize your serious commitment. (Yes, many people will question your motives and think you are just trying to build your résumé.)

Getting an appointment can be difficult because politicians and community leaders are busy people and their agendas are usually booked for weeks in advance. If you succeed in scheduling a meeting, don't be surprised if it gets canceled at the last minute. So, call ahead to confirm the time and place of the meeting. If your meeting does get canceled, try to meet with a member of the official's staff instead. Talking with an aide can actually be just as useful. Staff assistants are the real worker bees and often know more about the important issues than the elected officials. An aide can also act as a go-between and may be able to convince his/her boss that your ideas deserve attention.

Before a scheduled meeting, plan how you and your teammates can have the most impact in a short amount of time. Sometimes, you'll only have about 10 to 15 minutes and you'll want to make the most of it.

CHOOSE A CAPTAIN. *If you decide to bring a group of teammates and other supporters, limit this delegation to no more than five people. Select a "captain" to lead the conversation and assign each person specific points to talk about.*

STAY SPECIFIC. *Limit your discussion to one issue. Be very clear about what you want the power-holder to consider.*

BE FIRM, BUT UNDERSTANDING. *Avoid placing unreasonable demands on public officials. They will need to be convinced that your idea is worthy and, even more importantly, that supporting your initiative will not make too many enemies.*

BRING WRITTEN MATERIAL. *Prepare a folder with fact sheets and other evidence (graphs, photographs, etc.) that may be eye-catching and will support your argument. A clever tactic you can use is to summarize your key points and background information into a small pamphlet (the size of a business envelope) that a politician can keep in his/her pocket and review during floor debate or before an important vote.*

PUT YOURSELF IN THEIR SHOES. *Think about what it would take to change their mind. Besides statistics, you might want to interest policy-makers by mentioning how your initiative could benefit them and their families. Sometimes you might need to get personal and appeal to their sense of right and wrong.*

RESPOND TO QUESTIONS DIRECTLY. *If you are asked a real stumper of a question, don't wing it. Answer by saying either that you haven't looked at that aspect of the issue yet or that you'll get back to them later with a response. Even if there is no follow-up information to send, a personal thank-you card can help to cement the memory of your meeting in the mind of a VIP or a staff assistant.*

BE CONFIDENT. *Firm handshakes are important. Look them in the eye. It's normal to feel intimidated by important people, but remember, "they put their pants on one leg at a time, too!"*

THANK THEM. *Be polite by thanking them for their time and make sure to jot down the names of any staff aides at the meeting, since they may be the ones you will want to contact again later.*

MEETING WITH LAWMAKERS

If you want to meet with a state lawmaker or member of Congress, it doesn't require traveling to the statehouse or the U.S. Capitol. Every legislator has at least one local district office. Usually a call to directory assistance or looking in the telephone book will give you the information to get started.

Many elected officials also hold town meetings. These forums provide an opportunity for citizens to speak their minds. Try to attend one, if you can. You may even be able to exchange a few words before or after the event, which might result in an invitation to come by and meet with the official later on.

GETTING THE "BRUSH OFF"

Just because you are young does not mean that you should not be taken seriously. Getting the "brush off" can be expected, but it shouldn't be tolerated, accepted or excused. In such cases, keep your cool and remain polite, even if you and your group feel under attack. Stick up in defense of yourself and your ideas. If you are treated rudely and you are certain that this decision-maker will remain a fierce opponent, consider publicizing your encounter by writing a guest article for the city newspaper or giving a scoop to a television station. Most would advise you never to burn bridges, but this sort of public shaming can mobilize community support and increase the pressure — sometimes causing elected officials to change their minds.

Of course, meetings are only one aspect of face-time. There will be occasions when it will be important that others see you, for instance at a news conference or a rally. Also remember that you can testify at public hearings conducted by local and state legislative committees (for more information, see the next chapter). Most school boards and many city councils set aside time at every meeting for an open forum allowing **concerned citizens** to speak briefly about any issue. In some places, public officials have also instituted regular sessions with ordinary folks such as "Meet the Mayor." If no open door program exists in your community, you might want to propose such an idea. **Face-to-face meetings can make a lasting impression** and help you gain support. So, go out there and be seen!

STAND UP (OR SIT DOWN) FOR WHAT YOU BELIEVE IN

Your team will likely be competing with many other local leaders and organized groups that are pursuing issues of their own, so it may be difficult to get noticed. If letters, petitions, and face-to-face meetings do not attract the attention you had expected, then it's time to try **other tactics**, especially those that mobilize large numbers of people. **Numbers count,** and events that draw large crowds command respect.

For example, governors, mayors and school boards usually hold large conferences or summits when they want to get input from citizens about pressing issues and concerns. However, there is no reason that you cannot stage a similar meeting in which citizens speak out about how they feel regarding a particular problem or proposal. Get people from all across your city or state to attend and invite a few key decision-makers to speak. Make sure the agenda is organized so these VIPs can hear some of your group's concerns and proposals. Your public officials will leave with an earful and a better sense of what their constituents want.

Similarly, **a march or rally** has the potential of raising awareness about a problem—not just among politicians and business leaders, but throughout your community. A silent candlelight vigil will focus attention on a serious problem that remains unnoticed or ignored. Human billboarding using sandwich board posters or banners at busy intersections may be unusual or creative enough to make the evening news. These and other methods of protesting, although considered extreme by some, can be just the thing to pressure certain individuals or institutions to respond. A word of warning, though: public demonstrations sometimes run the risk of doing more harm than good. Weigh the pros and cons carefully before you decide to "take to the streets."

To ensure that your event makes a positive impact, give yourself twice as much time to prepare as you think is needed. Although many summits or rallies appear to be spontaneous gatherings, successful ones have been carefully planned. In addition, consider . . .

VOIDING THE COMPETITION:

Make sure an event will not conflict with exams, homecoming or other school activities. Find out about other community events, such as concerts or a march, by calling the Chamber of Commerce or Visitor's Bureau. The police department can also tell you what permits have been approved for parades, festivals, and rallies on specific dates.

OCATION:

Pick a good spot to illustrate your concern. It might be in front of a rundown community center or the site of a proposed landfill. An unfamiliar area can keep away supporters as well as the news media. On the other hand, a central location will attract curious onlookers.

TIMING:

If the purpose of a rally is a wake-up call to the community, schedule it for the convenience of your supporters and the news media, perhaps after school, but before the evening news. If your goal is to influence a vote, the ideal time may be right before the "yeas" and "nays" are taken. However, because the schedule for the school board or state legislature can be difficult to predict, your best bet is to plan a demonstration **whenever decision-makers will be around** so supporters can have the opportunity to lobby them in person.

PERMITS:

Check well in advance with the police department or the appropriate government agency about a permit. Inquire about any local restrictions, such as a noise ordinance at parks. If you run into roadblocks, contact the local office of the American Civil Liberties Union. ACLU members can advise you of your rights and help you deal with possible obstacles.

TRANSPORTATION:

Try to rely on public mass transportation. Otherwise, rides, carpools and other transportation to and from the event should be well organized and publicized in order to get a strong turnout. Someone on your team may even want to arrange for buses to run back and forth between the site of your event and a central location.

SPEAKERS:

A prominent political figure or **celebrity** can attract a crowd as well as the media. A key decision-maker, such as a school board member or state legislator who has been your strongest supporter, can add legitimacy to a youth-run rally and definitely should be invited to speak.

YOUTH!

OTHER ATTRACTIONS:

Singers and other entertainment can **liven up the event**. Chants and slogans enhance the spirit and unity of the crowd. Of course, a reliable sound system is essential. Banners and posters reinforce the message as do symbolic props. At one rally, students carried an empty coffin in support of tougher drunk driving legislation.

NEWS MEDIA:

Mail or fax a news release two weeks before the event. Follow up with phone calls. Decide ahead of time who will be the official spokespeople. See if a few stations will broadcast a 20-second public service announcement promoting the vigil or march. On the day of the event, make early morning **reminder calls** to newspapers, radio and television stations.

CROWD CONTROL:

A clear standard of behavior should be made known to everyone involved. Based on the size of the crowd expected, a handful of people should also be responsible for making sure things don't get out of hand. Prior to a march, those who volunteer to be marshals should receive training on how to respond to hecklers and police. Counter-protesters can turn a peaceful demonstration into a violent one. If you anticipate the likelihood of trouble, consider hiring off-duty police officers to provide security.

SYMBOLIC PROPS AND VISUALS

A guest speaker planted the idea in the minds of some students at Provo High School, Utah, that they should take the lead on lobbying for a statewide smoking ban in most public places. This club got 22 other schools to join in a huge rally at the state capitol. Their banners read, "I Want Fresh Air," translated into 30 different languages. A certain percentage of students painted their faces white to "symbolize those who have died from secondhand smoke." In addition, students gave every legislator an air freshener. It worked. Legislation that had been defeated for the past three years became law.

26% at work

NUMBERS COUNT

Students in Connecticut informed the news media ahead of time, but surprised the Mayor by walking to his home to demand that funds be restored for a community recreation center in downtown Bridgeport. With the presence of TV cameras, the Mayor agreed to change the city budget and provide money for youth services.

Civil disobedience is a giant step beyond the various public demonstrations noted above. There are serious consequences for **deliberately** breaking the law in order to challenge it, including school expulsion and arrest. Definitely seek guidance from experienced activists and parents if you do consider such a tactic. In addition, it would be a smart idea to get some coaching on how to respond to difficult situations that might arise.

Likewise, it will also be necessary to launch a **public awareness campaign** so that everyone understands why you are doing what you feel must be done. There are ways to avoid a negative public backlash. From the early days of your campaign, call reporters and write letters to the editor. Make sure people know of your repeated efforts to talk with the powers-that-be. If you then decide to demonstrate, your public record will make it more difficult for critics to suggest your group is impatient, unreasonable, or acting irresponsibly. A walk-out at school or a sit-in at city hall is more likely to gain public approval if it is known that you tried over and over again to meet with public officials to negotiate. Picketing a business for its discriminatory treatment of teens will win more support if customers and bystanders receive leaflets that document a pattern of such incidents.

YOUTH!

ROCK THE VOTE *NOW!*

You don't have to wait until you are 18 to be active in electoral politics. Lots of opportunities exist for you now. Some approaches are traditional, like being a campaign volunteer, while others are new and innovative. Some may not even be thought of yet and await your creative spirit and energy. The point is, if you want to make your voice heard in an election, don't think the voting booth is the only way. Our democracy depends on **people of all ages** to participate in politics year round, not just in November.

BE A CAMPAIGN VOLUNTEER.

Whether the candidate is seeking a seat on the school board or state legislature, or even the office of Governor or President, he/she will need your help. Many campaigns depend on people who give their time and effort. You can distribute leaflets, pass out lawn signs, register people to vote, or pitch in at local polling places. Most politicians will value your support, especially knowing that soon you will be a full-fledged constituent. They also recognize the influence you may have on the voting decisions of older friends and family members.

START A BALLOT INITIATIVE.

In more than a dozen states and in many local areas, proposals and public questions can be placed on the ballot for voters to decide. In many instances, all you have to do is collect a certain number of signatures and the item will appear on the ballot. Other times, the state legislature has to decide if issues can be brought to referendum. If you have an idea, talk with officials at the local elections bureau or contact your legislator. You might be able to offer an idea for a ballot initiative or support an issue going to referendum.

POWER WITHOUT THE VOTE

26% at work

More than 10,000 students in Los Angeles walked out of classes in 1994 to demonstrate against a California referendum barring illegal immigrants from attending schools and receiving other public services. Leonardo Hernandez, 16, who was among the Montebello High School demonstrators said, "Maybe if they see us, people will realize that this is what will happen if the proposition passes because we will all be in the streets instead of school."

THE 26% SOLUTION

HOLD A CANDIDATES' FORUM. Another option for you is to hold a candidates' forum in which young people—rather than adults and reporters—get the opportunity to question those running for school board or local government. Have a panel of student questioners, but invite the entire community. Because of your knowledge about certain issues and the candidates' positions, you may be much better informed than many voters, who will ultimately benefit from hearing your concerns and the candidates' responses. So let them.

RATE THE CANDIDATES. Anyone, regardless of age, can judge the candidates. Student associations, environmental groups, and numerous other advocacy organizations usually rate the candidates based on their campaign promises, past voting records, and contributors to their campaign. So, do some research and form an opinion. Publicize your views about candidates through editorials in the school newspaper and submit a guest article or letter to the editor of daily and weekly newspapers. Your thoughts about the candidates can influence how others vote.

To obtain non-partisan information about local and state races, rely on the local chapter of the League of Women Voters. Voting records, accounts of campaign contributions, and other factual information on all those running for the U.S. Congress are available free of charge from Project Vote Smart. *(See pages 82-83.)*

MOCK ELECTIONS. Concern about low voter turnout, especially among those between the ages of 18 and 24, has increased the popularity of programs such as Kids Voting and other mock elections that are designed to get young people in the habit of turning out on election day. In addition to providing an opportunity to vote for candidates and local and state referenda, a new approach has been to include ballot questions on issues of primary concern to young people. Often these mock elections are held prior to election day, so that voters, as well as politicians, know how thousands of young people feel about the issues through their "votes."

YOUTH!

LOWER THE VOTING AGE?

Proposals to lower the voting age surface from time to time in Oregon and other states. No sustained campaign has yet materialized, but that does not mean one day it won't happen. One legislative proposal in Minnesota may stand a pretty good chance. If passed, it would allow 16-year-olds to vote in school board elections. Currently, high school students in hundreds of school districts across the country only vote for the student board member who serves on the local board of education.

Even without power at the voting booth, those under the age of 18 can still have considerable influence on the voters and the candidates. And once you're eligible to vote, get out and do so, but remember about all the other things you can do. You might even consider running for office. The student representative of the Hawaii Board of Education graduated and then won a seat on the school board as an adult member. A 17-year-old student got 38% of the vote in his bid to unseat the Mayor of Hesston, Kansas, who happened to be his high school government teacher. At age 19, Marcus Molinara won the mayoral election in Tivoli, New York. You can make a difference at any age.

YOUTH VOTE

California's Marin County Youth Commission ran a mock election at dozens of high schools and included 15 ballot questions including "Which of the following would be most effective in reducing youth crime and violence?" This was not purely an educational exercise. The results were widely publicized with the goal of influencing policy-makers at the county and state levels.

26% at work

Marin County Youth VOTE '96—Sample Ballot

Please punch out the appropriate answer on your voting machine. Please be sure the question and number on the card in the machine match the question and number in the voting booklet.

NOTE: If you're not in touch with the candidates or issues, please refer to the candidates' statements and ballot arguments in the back pages of the booklet.

Presidential Election

President of the United States
*(Choose only **one**)*

3. *Candidate of the American Independent Party*
4. Bill Clinton, *Democratic P...*
5. Ralph Nader, *Green ...*
6. Harry Brown,...
7. *Candid...*
8. *C... P...*
9. R...
10. Bob...

State-Ba...

I. Should regulations be enacted to restrict campaign contributions and spending?

13. Yes
14. No

II. Should the California Civil Rights Initiative be passed?

15. Yes
16. No

V. Should the minimum wage be raised from $4.25 per hour to $5.75 in California?

17. Yes
18. No

V. Should California legalize marijuana for medicinal purposes?

19. Yes
... No

...lifornia pass consumer
...garding the practices of healt...

...Youth Vote Issues

...hould the U.S. Congress amend the 1973 federal Endangered Species Act to allow for some alteration of the habitats of endangered species during the course of development?

29. Yes
30. No

VIII. Do you feel that a young woman under the age of 18 should be required to obtain the consent of one parent (or legal guardian) before getting an abortion?

31. Yes
32. No

IX. Should public schools offer bilingual education programs to students whose native language is not English?

33. Yes
34. No

5

INFO Starters VOTING
See also page 47.

KIDS VOTING USA
398 South Mill Avenue
Tempe AZ 85281
602-921-3727
www.kidsvoting.org

LEAGUE OF WOMEN VOTERS
1730 M Street NW #1000
Washington DC 20036
800-249-VOTE
www.lwv.org

Marin County Youth VOTE '96—Sample Ballot

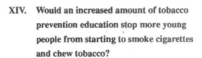

X. Should the California State Government allocate more money to the public school system?

35. Yes
36. No

XI. What areas of the California public school system do you feel need the most improvement? *(Mark up to five answers)*

37. Decrease in class size
38. Books
39. Classroom materials
40. Fine arts education
41. Sports programs
42. Campus renovations
43. Technology
44. Counselors
45. Teachers' salaries
46. Bilingual education
47. New schools built
48. Drug, alcohol, tobacco and violence prevention classes
50. College prep classes
51. Vocational education
52. No improvement is needed

XII. Do you think that the cost of a college education in California will prevent you from attending the college of your choice?

55. Yes
56. No

XIII. Should HIV/AIDS education be taught in fifth and sixth grade?

57. Yes
58. No

XIV. Would an increased amount of tobacco prevention education stop more young people from starting to smoke cigarettes and chew tobacco?

59. Yes
60. No

XV. Which of the following would be *most effective* in reducing youth crime and violence? *(Choose only two)*

61. *Curfews*
62. *Increase positive alternatives for youth:* employment and job training opportunities; community activities for youth; youth development programs.
64. *Build stronger relationships between young people and community adults:* youth and parents, youth and police, connecting young people to positive mentors, etc.
66. *Stricter penalties and sentencing:* try youth in adult courts; "three-strikes-and-you're-out" laws.
68. *Increase programs which target juvenile offenders for rehabilitation and treatment.*

Elections—Marin County

XVI. U.S. House of Representatives
(Choose only one)

82. Lynn Woolsey, Democratic Party
83. Bruce Kendall, *Natural Law Party*
84. Ernest K. Jones, *Peace and Freedom Party*
85. Duane Hughes, *Republican Party*

NATIONAL STUDENT/PARENT
MOCK ELECTION
225 West Oro Valley Drive
Tucson AZ 85737
* Send a stamped self-addressed
envelope for information.

PROJECT VOTE SMART
129 NW Fourth Street #240
Corvallis OR 97330
800-622-SMART
www.oclc.org/VoteSmart

ROCK THE VOTE
10635 Santa Monica Blvd.
Los Angeles, CA 90025
310-234-0665
www.rockthevote.org

C H A P T E R   4
Strategies for Influencing Decision-Makers

We hope you are convinced that **your influence extends beyond your own peer group** and that important people will listen to you. Now is the time to put your energy into persuading key individuals to pay attention and respond to your ideas. This chapter will outline a number of strategies that are effective when dealing with different audiences, particularly school officials and administrators, business people, community leaders, and local and state politicians. Each section offers an integrated approach that combines what we have already described with some new material. As always, a few hints and some success stories are included for you to ponder.

A Class Act
IMPROVING SCHOOLS FOR STUDENTS

In initiating change at your school, your principal can be your best friend or your worst enemy, because — like it or not — you're stepping on his/her turf. Whether things work out favorably or not depends in part on how much the administration is committed to improving your school, and the extent to which it values student input and participation in this process. It is up to you to be convincing and show that your suggestions will ensure improvements that will not only benefit your fellow students and the school community, but will make your school look good. If you are successful, you can be certain that your principal will seek you out for help in the future.

However, if your principal is less than supportive or is not the one able to make the change, you may have to look higher up the ladder, to the superintendent or a group of elected or appointed people known as the board of education. Some reforms, especially those involving more than one school, the distribution of funds for programs, and new policies, are decided at this level. In some cases, though, decisions about how schools are run may be made by the county council, the state board of education, or your state legislature.

In all 50 states and the District of Columbia, the state board of education votes on certain policies and requirements for all students and schools. Typically, they can decide the length of the school year and school day, minimum requirements for graduation, mandatory testing, funding levels for school construction, even whether a student's driver's license can be revoked for failing to maintain a certain grade point average. Sometimes, the state superintendent of schools and the state board of education study various proposals and make recommendations to the state legislature.

Usually there about a dozen people, including teachers and parents on the state school board, who are appointed by the governor. A growing number of states also have a student member seated with their state school board, including Alaska, Hawaii, Minnesota, Montana, Nevada, North Carolina and Tennessee. Connecticut and Washington have two student board members and the student board members of California, Maryland, and Massachusetts have voting rights. Most of these students are chosen by the governor based on the recommendation of the state student council association. This trend to involve students in the decision-making process is due partly to many adults who realize the benefit of getting input from the education "consumers"—those who know firsthand about what's going on in the classroom. Across the country, hundreds of students now sit on local school boards, as well. Many big city school districts—from Jackson, Mississippi, to the Los Angeles Unified School District, and also including those in rural and suburban areas—have one or two elected student board members.

STUDENT SAVES SCHOOL SYSTEM $100,000

The Anne Arundel County School Board in Maryland has paid serious attention to the advice of its student representatives, each of whom has enjoyed full voting rights since 1975. The McGill Plan, named after the student school board member who proposed modifying the bus schedule during high school mid-term and final exams, has saved this school district $100,000 annually.

26% at work

HOW TO WIN STUDENT REPRESENTATION

If your school district doesn't already have at least one student member on the school board, you can start the ball rolling. Organize a group and conduct a poll or petition drive to see how many of your peers approve of the idea. Be sure to educate people about your reasons for supporting this action. Put together and then distribute a fact sheet. **Collect endorsements** from your student council, other student and school organizations, teachers, principals, the PTA, community groups, etc. Publicize your campaign to the local news media.

Next, you should **meet with individual school board members** and seek their support to expand the board to include one or two students. Find at least one influential member who is willing to sponsor your proposal. Recruit students from other schools representing different geographical regions in the school district who can lobby their own board members. Meanwhile, your group can **select a student liaison to the school board.** This person can take on the role as an unofficial student representative and continually bring student perspectives and issues to the attention of the school board. Also, work to get student members appointed to various school committees and task forces. Your goal is to show adult

YOUTH!

members what a student member can do and how important it is to get input from students. This short-term strategy can help gain acceptance of the concept of representation.

As always, get your supporters to **write letters, make telephone calls, and testify before the school board.**
Make sure the news media know about your campaign. Also, be prepared to compromise—perhaps you will need to agree to start with a non-voting student member at first. In time, the position can be reevaluated and more responsibility can be added, such as the right to vote on certain proposals (usually not on budget, personnel and legal matters). In many school districts, approval by the state legislature is required. Other times, a student member can be included by a simple vote of the school board through a change in its policy or bylaws.

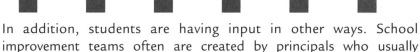

In addition, students are having input in other ways. School improvement teams often are created by principals who usually appoint students from each grade. At the school district level, the superintendent may form an advisory committee to make recommendations on how to reduce racial tension or strengthen the intramural sports program. Also, committees responsible for developing new curriculum or revising disciplinary policies no longer rely solely on school administrators and other professionals, but people of all ages. Students frequently are included and, in some cases, outnumber adults.

There are many ways for you to speak up about education issues. Talk with your principal or assistant principal. Get a group of your friends together and **attend a school board meeting**. Seek out the student board member or other board members. Make a phone call or write a letter. If you are interested in serving on an advisory committee, don't keep it a secret. Ask to be appointed. Better yet, push for more student representation on all committees including your local and state board of education.

Making your ideas a reality usually requires winning support one member at a time. Not everyone has to be convinced. All you need is a majority to vote "yes."

YOUTH INFLUENCING EDUCATION

(See Chapter 2: Over 100 National Organizations & Clearinghouses)

The following organizations can provide information on student involvement with boards of education, school committees, and education task forces across the country.

INTERNATIONAL STUDENT ACTIVISM ALLIANCE
31 North Quaker Lane
West Hartford CT 06119-0287
860-232-8452
e-mail: CCLUF@aol.com
www.avonct.com/isaa
This youth-run organization, with over 100 chapters nationwide, advocates for student board members and also is active on a wide range of student rights and academic issues.

NATIONAL ASSOCIATION OF INDEPENDENT SCHOOLS
1601 L Street
Washington DC 20036
202-973-9700
www.nais-schools.org
This organization serves as a clearinghouse for private schools.

NATIONAL ASSOCIATION OF STATE BOARDS OF EDUCATION
1012 Cameron Street
Alexandria VA 22314
703-684-4000
www.nasbe.org
This national clearinghouse concentrates on providing information and technical assistance to the student as well as adult members of the state school boards.

NATIONAL ASSOCIATION OF STUDENT COUNCILS
c/o National Association of Secondary School Principals
1904 Association Drive
Reston VA 22091
703-860-0200 ext. 336
www.nassp.org
Most states have a state student council association that works on student issues like youth representation and education. For more information and to find out the names and phone numbers of your state advisor and president, contact the NASC office. Also check with your school student council advisor, who can help you get on the right track. Secondary school student councils can affiliate with the state and national organizations. See if your school is a member and receives any services, such as information, resources, or student leadership training, which may be offered.

NATIONAL SCHOOL BOARDS ASSOCIATION
1680 Duke Street
Alexandria VA 22314
703-838-6731
www.nsba.org
This organization and its library provide information on model programs, education trends and

statistics in rural, suburban and urban public school systems throughout the country.

STUDENT LEADERSHIP NETWORK
202 South State Street, #1400
Chicago IL 60604
866-LEADER-3
www.studentleaders.org
This youth-run organization primarily concentrates on education issues and student representation.

YOUTH ON BOARD
PO Box 440322
Somerville MA 02144
617-623-9900
www.youthonboard.org
This national organization provides assistance and training to both student and adult members serving on school boards as well as other boards of directors.

STUDENTS ARE "SEEN AND HEARD" BY SCHOOL BOARDS

"It's a matter of telling as many people as you can. Speak at the formal public meeting of the School Board. Get it out in the open. Most important, be specific about what needs to be changed."
- High school senior Kendell Kelly of Maryland, who persuaded the school board to replace her principal and agree to other student proposals to reduce the escalating school violence after a classmate was killed on campus.

The Idaho Board of Education held town meetings around the state on a proposal to no longer require students to take health education and P.E.

Corey Christensen and other students enrolled in a Health Occupations class created a petition and in one day, collected 394 signatures. Over 200 showed up for the hearing, along with teachers and parents. Corey made an impassioned speech to preserve the existing graduation requirements and the School-to-Work program.

26% at work

YOUTH!

Letter to school Superintendent

Letter
Superintendent
Superintendent

S.O.S. Students Oppose Smoking — *A County-wide student led effort to Save Our Schools*

saveourschools@hotmail.com

March 27, 1996

Dr. Paul Vance
Superintendent of Schools
850 Hungerford Drive
Rockville, Maryland 20850

Dear Dr. Vance:

Students Oppose Smoking - Save Our Schools (S.O.S.) requests your presence and participation at an important student-led press conference on Monday, April 22, 1996, 9:30 a.m. to be held at Albert Einstein High School (Northwood), 919 University Boulevard.

Students Oppose Smoking is an organization established by Montgomery County high school students representing all regions of our county. In 1994, almost thirty percent of the _____ welfth graders were smoking. The biggest increase of _____ females. These numbers are much too high. Our long _____ rette smoking and the use of tobacco products by _____ ctive is to stop smoking in and around our schools.

_____ Oppose Smoking is organizing a major press _____ widespread school problem. Our concerted effort, _____ wspaper reporters from at least twelve county high _____ tion on smoking in our schools and the numerous _____ ts, especially nonsmokers, as well as faculty

_____ ns for resolution to these issues. That will include _____ hat we would like to see implemented before the _____ ue your participation and reactions to our _____ onference. Your presence is greatly needed so _____ serious health problem which is of epidemic _____ ry County.

_____ ndy Norcross at (301) 929-8550. We know you _____ e hope you will make the time to attend.

_____ y High School)

Flyer for youth forum

youth
youth

SPEAK OUT!!

FORUM ON SCHOOL POLICIES

Uniforms, Homework & Attendance

Tell PAUL VALLAS, MAYOR DALEY & THE BOARD OF TRUSTEES WHAT YOU THINK!

MONDAY, FEBRUARY 10, 1997

4:30pm - 6:00pm

Lots of space to SPEAK OUT

Meet MIGUEL AYALA, Student Member to the Chicago Board of Trustees!

Roosevelt University, 2nd Floor
430 South Michigan Ave
(downtown, on the corner of Congress & Michigan)

ALL STUDENTS INVITED!

We'll have a panel of students (including Miguel Ayala, Student Member on the Board of Trustees) and adults (including school officials) to answer your questions about school policies and how you can change them. Tell them which policies work in your school and which ones have to go!

FREE PIZZA & CTA TOKENS

Tell us you're coming! Call Heather at Student Alliance at (312) 922-5150

Speak Out is a forum for elementary and high school students to address issues that are important to them. Speak Out is sponsored by Student Alliance, the city's only student-run organization. If you would like a membership application to Student Alliance or to volunteer, call us at (312) 922-5150 or visit us online at http://www.studentalliance.org. Special thanks to CENtel, Roosevelt University and the WPWR-TV Channel 50 Foundation for making Speak Out possible!

[Map: Student Alliance 28 East Jackson; Jackson; RED LINE "LOOP 'L'"; Van Buren; Roosevelt University; Congress; Michigan; 430 South Michigan, 2nd; Wabash; State]

Close To Home
INFLUENCING CITY HALL AND YOUR COUNTY GOVERNMENT

Thanks to community cable access and the Internet, it's a whole lot easier to see what's going on at your town hall or county government. You don't even need to leave home in order to learn what issues are being debated by local decision-makers. Just a click of the remote control or your computer's mouse, and you can find out easily whether an effort is underway to expand a recycling program or to overturn the existing curfew for minors. Your local government is incredibly accessible.

Unless you live in Chicago, New York, or some other huge city, it is likely that you'll find only a dozen or so key elected decision-makers who make up your local government. You may have a city or town representative, who might be called council member, commissioner, supervisor, selectman, or alderman. Or, if you live in a rural area, you might have a county council or board of county commissioners. Some areas have both a city government and county government where each has different responsibilities over police, parks, restaurants, roads, mass transportation, libraries, the environment— even tattoo parlors. Voters may also elect a mayor or county executive and council members, or the elected members of your council may appoint a city manager.

"Think Globally, Act Locally"

Twelve-year-old Andrew Holleman of Massachusetts succeeded in stopping a developer from building a 180-unit condominium in his favorite woods. One of his winning tactics was voicing his concerns to the board of health, conservation commission, and zoning board on how construction could destroy this wildlife habitat and also how sewage from the housing complex could contaminate the underground wells that provide the town's drinking water.

26% at work

Unlike most state legislatures that only meet for several months and may be located hundreds of miles away, your local government works year round and is nearby. This means there are more opportunities for you to bring issues and concerns to these decision-makers or to the many local government departments, agencies, and commissions that also have considerable power to influence and actually set policies. In addition, there are a number of **special task forces** at this level that have been created to study particular problems and recommend solutions. Such committees are made up of concerned citizens and may also have a youth representative. Find

Enlist the Young

Tell it to the Mayor!

If Mayor Giuliani wants the city to work, he'll need New York City's young people as his allies.

In each division of the administration, from the Office for Children and Families to the Department of Juvenile Justice, he could start by establishing positions for student representatives.

It is not enough to assume that his offices are responding to young people's needs; young policy makers themselves would be in the best position to know which policies work and which don't. Besides, they'll be smart and energetic and won't be beholden to special interests the way politicians are.

By considering young people a constituency worthy of his attention, Mr. Giuliani will also be reaching out to their parents, teachers and communities.

— *ANDREA SCHLESINGER, student advisory member on the Board of Education*

out. It is increasingly common for young people to be appointed to many of these citizen committees and some town councils are even expanding their own membership to include a non-voting youth representative or a separate youth advisory council.

If you have an idea on how to tackle a problem, want to propose a new local law, or think an existing ordinance should be repealed, you can start close to home.
Here are a few strategies to begin this process.

1 FIND OUT WHO's WHO. Check the blue pages of your telephone book and contact the town, city, or county council office. See if there is a Web site that will familiarize you with the names of individual members, as well as the names of certain departments and agencies and what they are responsible for. If not, you might want to request that a brochure containing this information be sent to you.

2 TALK WITH THE CLERK. Call the clerk of the council and ask whether the issue you are concerned about is currently being considered. If so, ask how you can get copies of any proposals (often called ordinances or bills). If the issue isn't being discussed, you can bring it up. Ask which committee has responsibility for the issue and get the name and phone number of the appropriate staff person.

3 CONTACT THE STAFF. Talk with the person in charge of a particular issue to learn more about pending proposals on this subject and what action has occurred in the past. Ask whether there is a special task force, commission, or board responsible for making recommendations on the issue that concerns you.

4 PUT TOGETHER YOUR ARGUMENTS. Continue your research and plan to share with local decision-makers the information you have compiled. Find out what other towns or cities have done and if they are pursuing solutions similar to what you are proposing *(refer to the organizations listed later under "INFO STARTERS" and also in Chapter 2).*

5 REQUEST A MEETING. Set up a time to visit with your own council member or his/her staff to discuss the issue and ask for their help, possibly asking them to introduce a proposal. If the council member is not supportive, seek out other local lawmakers, perhaps the chair of the committee responsible for considering the proposal.

6 CALL FREQUENTLY. Keep in contact with this council member and his/her aides and ask them to suggest which other council members should be lobbied.

7 MOBILIZE OTHERS. Recruit classmates, friends, neighbors, teachers, and other adults to play "constituent" and contact their own city or county council members, urging them to support your idea. Also, depend on your supporters. Ask your allies to keep urging other council members to support your proposal.

YOUTH!

8 PUBLICIZE. Send out a news release, call the radio and TV stations, and submit articles to the newspapers or letters to the editor.

9 FOLLOW UP. Continue to check in with those council members who remain undecided about whether or not to support your proposal. Be prepared to meet with individual council members and possibly the mayor or county executive.

10 TESTIFY. Make sure to speak at public hearings on your proposal and competing proposals. *(See page 106.)*

11 INVESTIGATE. Follow alternative proposals and amendments and be prepared to compromise. *(More on this in Chapter 5.)*

12 BE PERSISTENT! Don't give up.

Once an ordinance is passed in one town it may prompt other local governments to pass similar laws. Sometimes, this **snowball** effect prompts a legislature to take action statewide.

INFO Starters

YOUTH IN GOVERNMENT

ASSOCIATION OF YOUTH COUNCILS
2756 South Adams
South Salt Lake City UT 84115
801-487-5822
e-mail: gsession@burgoyne.com
www.ayc.org

COMMUNITY PARTNERSHIPS WITH YOUTH
6319 Constitution Drive
Fort Wayne IN 46804
219-436-4402
www.cpyinc.com

INTERNATIONAL CITY/COUNCIL MANAGEMENT
ASSOCIATION
777 North Capitol Street
Washington DC 20002
202-289-4262
www.iccma.org

NATIONAL ASSOCIATION OF COUNTIES
440 First Street NW
Washington DC 20001
202-393-6226
www.naco.org

NATIONAL ASSOCIATION OF TOWNS AND
TOWNSHIPS
444 North Capitol Street NW
Washington DC 20001
202-624-3550
e-mail: nataat@sso.org

NATIONAL LEAGUE OF CITIES
1301 Pennsylvania Avenue NW
Washington DC 20004
202-626-3000
www.nlc.org

U.S. CONFERENCE OF MAYORS
1620 Eye Street NW
Washington DC 20006
202-293-7330
www.usmayors.com/uscm

YOUTH LEADERSHIP INSTITUTE
870 Market Street
San Francisco, CA 94102
415-397-2256
www.yli.org

The local chapter of the Student Coalition Against Tobacco (SCAT) wanted to change one aspect of the annual homecoming parade in Parkersburg, West Virginia. Armed with a photograph of a 17-year-old obtaining a can of smokeless tobacco from the Skoal booth and other evidence, SCAT convinced the City Council to adopt a resolution that prohibits tobacco ads or free samples of cigarettes or chew at all events held on city-owned or leased property.

LOCAL YOUTH-DRIVEN CAMPAIGNS GET RESULTS

Teen Think Tank, composed of 75 youth from the Urban League and a student newspaper group in South Bend, Indiana, launched a campaign called "It's My Neighborhood—No Shooting Allowed." They persuaded their city council to pass an ordinance requiring firearm owners to store their guns safely and take gun training classes. Gun advocates, however, successfully lobbied the state legislature to pass a bill overturning the local law.

IT'S YOUR BUSINESS, TOO

EXERCISING YOUR CLOUT WITH COMPANIES AND NON-PROFIT ORGANIZATIONS

People often overlook the role that companies and non-profit organizations can play in affecting laws, promoting safe and socially conscious behavior and practices, and sponsoring programs. Instead, many look to the government as being the source of all change or, at least, being in a position to make most of the decisions, when in fact it is not. Government is a major player, but not the only one. Now that collaboration is emphasized, it is common for government to work with businesses and community groups to solve problems, like air pollution or violence, and achieve shared goals. For example, school systems increasingly rely on corporate sponsors to support public education programs, and community organizations work with government agencies to run youth activities and provide services to the homeless and others who are less fortunate.

These partnerships provide you with additional opportunities to exercise your clout. **Don't restrict your efforts** just to the school board, local government, or state legislature. Target businesses and non-profit organizations, as well, and take your ideas and suggestions to them. See what they can do for you. If your team is pushing for more after-school "safe havens," talk with the United Way and see if they will increase their funding for youth programs or give you the money to do it yourself. The Rotary Club or another business roundtable might be the best bet if you are demanding more job opportunities in your community. The worst thing that can happen is they will say "no," and all that means is you should approach other private companies or non-profit groups instead.

Sometimes, your initiative may also mean bringing some **less-than-flattering feedback** to the attention of business and community leaders. It's possible that you may be upset about certain services or programs offered by a community organization, or believe they could be improved. Receiving second class treatment at a restaurant or store might cause you to take on the role of a consumer activist. Other concerns may also make you feel justified about registering a complaint or criticizing how things are run. A product released by one company may harm the environment or be produced using sweatshop labor. **Don't be shy. They will listen.** After all, who wants an unhappy customer? Businesses and community organizations care about the bottom line, as well as their public image.

To catch the attention of a store owner or the chief executive officer of a shopping mall or multinational company, try a combination of tactics:

CALL. Most businesses and non-profit organizations are listed in the phone book or yellow pages. Larger companies have toll-free customer hotlines, so use them. To find the phone number, call directory assistance at 1-800-555-1212.

MEET WITH THE MANAGER. Start with the person in charge at the local level. Listen to his/her response to your ideas or complaints, whichever you have. Find out the official company position. Sometimes, you may have to go a level higher in order to seek a satisfactory resolution of your issue or to challenge a company policy.

WRITE AND WRITE OFTEN. Send letters of complaint to the owner or the chief executive officer at the main company office. Get your friends and family to write also. As a last resort, if you feel as though you're getting the "brush off" or being ignored, write to these decision-makers at their home address, which may be tracked down by looking in the phone book or getting a copy of their company's articles of incorporation.

PUBLICIZE. Negative media attention can cause business and community leaders to do a turn-around, especially if it paints them in a bad light. Send out news releases about your campaign. Modify letters and submit them for publication as articles or letters to the editor.

FILE A COMPLAINT. You can register a formal complaint either with your Attorney General's office, the Equal Employment Opportunity Commission, or the Better Business Bureau. Business practices that are unsafe or violate people's rights are against the law and may result in legal action being taken against the company or organization.

BOYCOTT A PRODUCT. You may be forced to take more serious action and injure businesses and organizations where it really hurts — the pocketbook. Not buying certain products and persuading others to do the same will send a message. Even the threat of a boycott that is well publicized can get results. Once they begin to feel the pressure, they will respond and take steps to improve their reputation. (Similarly, fewer donations can cripple a non-profit group and make it more responsive to your demands.)

Not everything you do has to involve negative economic pressure. Positive collective action or incentives can be just as successful, especially when businesses and organizations are rewarded for being socially conscious and doing the right thing. Encourage people to shop at certain stores or eat at a particular restaurant. Highlight a community organization for its efforts to hire youth, eliminate waste, or protect the environment. Often such support can promote good business practices elsewhere and put pressure on competitors to adopt similar policies.

YOUTH!

Don't Like It, Don't Buy It

Students active with the youth-run international organization, "Free The Children," are lobbying for their coaches and school systems to stop buying soccer balls that have been hand-stitched by very young children in Asia. Lower profits and bad press may ultimately pressure manufacturers and other companies to stop these inhumane labor practices.

It's Worth Complaining

A few students in Philadelphia wrote a letter to an outdoor advertising company complaining about a billboard for Camel cigarettes that was near their school. Much to their amazement, the company responded and the tobacco ad vanished. In a suburb of Los Angeles, students also protested a cigarette billboard and met with the corporate executive. A local reporter caught wind of the story and within two weeks, it made network news.

A New Image

Teenagers in Eureka, California, did not like the atmosphere at a community health clinic where the receptionists seemed unfriendly, so they convinced the director to hire them for the front office. This change has reduced the reluctance of many girls to seek medical information and care at the clinic.

CONSUMER RIGHTS

INFO Starters

Also refer to Chapter 2: Over 100 National Organizations and Clearinghouses.

CONSUMERS FEDERATION OF AMERICA
1424 16th Street NW
Washington DC 20036
202-387-6121
This is one of the largest consumer advocacy organization in the country.

CO-OP AMERICA
1612 K Street
Washington DC 20006
202-331-8166
www.coopamerica.org
A list of ongoing consumer boycotts is available.

INFACT CAMPAIGN HEADQUARTERS
256 Hanover Street
Boston MA 02113
800-688-8797
www.infact.org
This national grassroots organization has a history of launching consumer boycotts against transnational corporations that allegedly are

involved in "life-threatening abuse." The current Tobacco Industry Campaign targets Philip Morris and RJR Nabisco to stop marketing cigarettes to children around the world.

PHILANTHROPIC RESEARCH INC.
1126 Professional Drive
Williamsburg VA 23185
757-229-4631
This private organization provides financial and program information on over 600,000 non-profit organizations and agencies.

A "CAPITOL" IDEA

BEING HEARD BY YOUR STATE LEGISLATORS

STUDENTS STAND OUT WHEN THEY SPEAK UP . . .

"I had such a good feeling getting the state legislators to listen to me. We were the only two teens who testified. My advice: don't read your speech, but speak from your head and heart."

— Sarah Porter of Maryland who helped close a loophole in the state law that now requires police to administer a drug and alcohol test to the driver at the site of a life-threatening car crash.

When it comes to the legislature, teenagers, like most people, think of themselves as tourists, not lobbyists. The assumption is that state representatives and senators only talk with the bigwigs.

Not so.

You don't need to be a top expert or the "hired gun" of a large company or organization in order to be heard. You don't even need to be of voting age. Whether you want to offer an idea for a law or voice your opposition to a proposed bill, there are many opportunities for you to participate in the legislative process. It is not difficult at all. All you need is what you already have—your knowledge about the issue, a little evidence, a few visuals, and your concern.

During each legislative session, representatives and senators consider bills on just about every imaginable subject from how much money your school district should receive to which pollutants can be discharged into the air. The ideas for most of these proposed laws come directly from local elected officials, business representatives, and other citizens who have special interests and concerns. Legislators don't have the time or knowledge to be experts on specific issues which is why **they depend so much on lobbyists and people like**

you for information and guidance. The legislative process is designed to weed out weak proposals since most laws have far-reaching impact, affecting everyone in the entire state. Out of a thousand or so bills introduced each session in every state capitol, only a hundred or so actually become law.

Don't feel as though you need to understand the complex and u n p r e d i c t a b l e process in order to make your voice heard.

The trick is to find a mentor. This insider can help you identify the several key legislators you will need to work with, keep you informed on what's happening and alert you to times when it will be important for you to be seen and heard. Such an ally might be one of your own state legislators, a member of his or her staff, or perhaps an experienced lobbyist who spends lots of time at the state capitol.

While not every state legislature follows the same rules and procedures, they are very similar. (Nebraska is unique, as it is the only unicameral legislature in the country.) The remainder of this section is dedicated to helping you understand those processes. "Legislative Lingo" translates many of the terms you will hear used. The following roadmap identifies critical times for you to plug into the process and suggests some strategies that work. Being familiar with the way proposed laws are considered will help you track the progress and outcomes of bills that you are interested in and locate resources, such as hearing schedules and copies of bills. This section is rounded out with a few helpful hints that you can use, should you decide to testify before a legislative committee. We have also included a copy of the testimony presented before a House committee by one of the authors at age 15, which helped get a law enacted in Maryland giving limited voting rights to the state student school board member.

LEGISLATIVE LINGO

ADOPT
to approve an amendment, committee report, motion, bill, etc.

AMENDMENT
substitute language or added language that changes a bill.

AUTHOR
the legislator who introduces the bill; also called the sponsor.

BILL
a proposal that is formally introduced for consideration by the legislature to create, change, or abolish a law.

CALENDAR
a list of bills in the order in which they will be debated and voted in both the House and Senate.

CHAIRPERSON
usually refers to the legislator who is a committee chair; this is a powerful position because the chair can decide if and when hearings and votes will occur on various bills.

CHAMBER
refers to either the House where all the Representatives (also called Delegates) or the Senators meet to debate and vote on bills.

COMMITTEE
Representatives are assigned to various House committees and Senators to separate Senate committees; all bills are referred to specific committees and many do not move beyond this stage of the process.

CONFERENCE COMMITTEE
a special committee composed of Representatives and Senators who meet to iron out all the differences between two similar bills passed by the two chambers (compromises are often made that may weaken or strengthen the bill).

CONSTITUENT
a resident of the district represented by an elected official.

COSPONSOR
a legislator from the same Chamber as the author (or sponsor) of a bill who helps champion the proposal.

DELEGATE
another name for Representative.

DELEGATION
all the Representatives and Senators from one county or region in the state.

DISTRICT
the geographical area represented by an elected official.

A B C D E F G H I J K L

YOUTH!

FIRST READING
the formal introduction of a bill when it is assigned a number and referred to a committee.

FLOOR
the area in the Chamber, either the House or Senate, where legislators debate and vote for or against specific bills and floor amendments.

HEARING
a committee meeting in which individuals present different points of view on specific bills.

MARK UP
committee members actually go through a bill line by line and propose changes.

MOTION
a parliamentary tactic to propose an action such as a motion for a committee to vote or to end floor debate.

PRESIDENT
the top leadership position in the Senate.

REPRESENTATIVE
a legislator in the House (sometimes called Delegate).

SECOND READING
after committee hearings and work sessions, a committee report is presented to the full House or Senate detailing committee actions on specific bills; committee and floor amendments may be added to a bill at this time.

SENATOR
a legislator in the Senate.

SINE DIE
the final adjournment; all bills that have not won passage in both Chambers die and have to be reintroduced in the next legislative session.

SPEAKER
the top leadership position in the House.

SPONSOR
the Representative or Senator who introduces a bill and is chief champion of the proposed legislation.

THIRD READING
final debate on a bill which is followed by a vote for final passage.

WORK SESSION
a committee meeting when members consider legislative proposals and often mark up bills.

VETO
when the Governor (or President, in cases of legislation passed by the US Congress) does not sign a bill so it cannot become law.

MOVING YOUR PROPOSAL THROUGH THE LEGISLATURE

Most state legislatures convene in **January,** so start early. If you have an I D E A F O R A N E W L A W you should definitely arrange to meet with several of the legislators from your region before the session begins. Prior to setting up a meeting, find out whether a similar bill has been considered in the past and perhaps talk to a lobbyist who can give you some tips on how best to approach individual lawmakers. You can also see about talking with the chairperson of the committee that would be responsible for this proposed legislation.

Once you have an idea for a new law...

☞ *research similar bills*
☞ *meet lawmakers*

Track all bills introduced that deal with your issue of concern. Call the toll-free number most state legislatures operate and ask to be connected with the Legislative Reference Office. You can also access the Web site. Very quickly, you can identify bill numbers, get free copies of legislative proposals, and find out which committees are responsible for these proposals. At this stage, communicate with the lawmakers who are sponsoring the bills you support and their legislative assistants.

The committee chair will schedule a hearing on your bill and similar proposals, sometimes with very little advance notice.

This is your big opportunity to be a witness and testify in favor of your bill (see "Testifying Tips" at the end of this section). You should bring supporters and arrange for other witnesses to speak at the hearing. Make sure to **alert the news media that you will be speaking.** If you are unable to make it, be sure to write a letter or fax a written statement to the committee clerk. If you are feeling especially creative, send a video of your speech to key members of the committee as well as to a few TV stations.

YOUTH!

Once the committee has heard from witnesses, members will "mark up" the legislation. Possible actions at the "work session" include: reporting the bill favorably, giving the bill a favorable report with amendments, giving it an unfavorable report, or no report.

How a bill exits a committee is important—anything less than a favorable or favorable with amendments report can mean legislative death—so continue lobbying members of the committee with letters, phone calls, faxes, scheduled meetings and impromptu visits. Let them know your position on the bill and whether you support any proposed amendments. Expect to compromise *(see page 114)*. Inform the news media of your efforts. **Lawmakers behave differently when they are being watched!**

A bill that receives a favorable committee report moves to the floor (either from the House committee to the House Chamber or from the Senate committee to the Senate Chamber). At the second reading, committee amendments may be attached to the bill, as well as amendments from the floor. Then the bill is read for the third time, debated, and voted on by all members of the Chamber. Before the final floor vote, mobilize supporters to telephone, fax, e-mail, and write their own legislators (only Representatives if the bill is in the House; only Senators if the bill is scheduled for a vote there). Well-timed public displays of support, such as rallies or press conferences, will also catch the attention of legislators and the media.

Be sure legislators see the support...
- ⊠ *fax, phone, e-mail, write*
- ❖ *public rallies*
- 🗐 *press conferences*

A bill that receives a majority vote in the Chamber where it was introduced goes to the second Chamber for consideration.

There, it receives a first reading and is assigned to a committee. Bills that move to the second Chamber usually retain their original number. The bill now is halfway through the legislative process, but this is no time to slack off. Maintain the momentum. Send articles to your local newspaper, talk to reporters, and keep the issue in the public eye, publicly thanking those lawmakers who voted for the bill.

The bill travels a similar route in the second Chamber: a committee hearing and possibly then a committee "mark up" or "work session."

7 A bill that survives this stage will be debated and voted on during the third reading. The home stretch is near. Watch out for those sneaky amendments. A short sentence or even the word "or" instead of "and" proposed by the opposition can transform a strong bill into a weak one or ruin its chance for passage. Be sure to activate your phone tree and maybe even take your fellow supporters to the state capitol to pay a friendly visit to Senators or Representatives and their staff.

8 If the bill passes the second Chamber—but in a different version from what was adopted by the first Chamber—then it will be sent to a conference committee.

This special committee composed of Representatives and Senators has to compromise and agree on identical language. Rely on key staff people and your inside ally to find out whether certain legislators need to hear from their constituents. The compromise bill must pass both Chambers. Otherwise it dies. During the final weeks of the session, the process becomes very unpredictable, so communicate frequently with your inside contacts.

9 The Governor has the last word, either signing the bill into law, allowing the bill to become law without a signature, or vetoing it. At this stage, the Governor may need an extra push, so send letters, e-mails, even telegrams.

Usually, the Governor has about two weeks to decide. If the bill is vetoed, the state legislature can override the veto by a two-thirds majority of both Chambers. This may be your last chance. In which case, pull out all the stops and make your views heard loud and clear. Otherwise, if a bill signing ceremony is in the works, NOW is the time to celebrate! See if you and others who helped push the bill through can attend.

YOUTH!

VICTORIOUS YOUTH-LED CAMPAIGNS

26% at work

Seventh graders in Dallas, Texas documented the number of liquor stores in their area, especially near schools. They traveled to the state legislature to present their findings. Senator West, a strong supporter, declared "The children motivated me. I'm going to do all I can to help get the bill passed." The law was changed to allow the local zoning board to reduce the number of liquor stores.

Seventeen-year-old runaway Janna Koschene of Colorado presented a vivid account of sleeping in cars and overnight shelters at a hearing conducted by a congressional committee. She gave detailed recommendations based on her own positive experiences at a drop-in center in Denver. At a time of budget cuts, Congress voted to spend more money for crisis shelters and other community-based youth centers.

Compelling testimony by young people based on their personal experiences of discrimination convinced Massachusetts legislators to pass the landmark Gay and Lesbian Student Rights Law. Students, with the support of the Lieutenant Governor, spoke at hearings, met with individual lawmakers, organized a massive letter-writing campaign, and held rallies and candlelight vigils that raised public support.

Trying to accomplish something at the state level can be a challenge. Expect several short, intense periods of involvement. One week you might be arranging for several people to miss school so that they can testify before a legislative committee, and the next you might be planning a rally on the steps of the statehouse. It promises to be a frustrating, yet fascinating adventure. Have fun and make history!

LAWMAKERS

STATE LAWMAKERS:

TOLL-FREE HOTLINES.
Find out if your state legislature operates a toll-free number that can connect you with any lawmaker, committee or legislative information office. Call directory assistance at 800-555-1212.

WEB SITES.
Search for the web site of your state legislature. Within seconds, you can find out all bills that have been introduced on a particular subject, for example, those proposals that would change the rules for driver's licenses. The bill sponsors, hearing dates, votes and other bill status information will appear on your computer screen. Many of these sites let you type in your zip code and within seconds, the names of all your state representatives and senators appear and, of course, in one key stroke, you can send them e-mail messages.

NATIONAL CONFERENCE OF
STATE LEGISLATORS
1560 Broadway
Denver CO 80202
303-830-2200
www.ncsl.org/public/siteleg.htm

NATIONAL LAWMAKERS:

HOUSE OF
REPRESENTATIVES
U.S. Congress
Washington DC 20515
202-224-3121
www.house.gov

SENATE
U.S. Congress
Washington DC 20510
202-224-3121
www.senate.gov

PRESIDENT
1600 Pennsylvania Avenue
Washington DC 20500
202-456-1414
www.whitehouse.gov

TESTIFYING TIPS

◆ THERE ARE NO INVITATIONS. Anyone can testify.

◆ PREPARE. If you or your group intend to speak at the committee hearing, begin planning before the hearing date is announced.

◆ EXCUSED ABSENCE. Figure out who can get out of school and make sure your parents and principal are aware of what you are doing.

◆ TRANSPORTATION. Decide who's driving and get a map (you don't want to get lost). Plan to get to the statehouse early so you can find a parking space and still have enough time to find the committee hearing room and get a seat in front.

YOUTH!

◆ CHECK COMMITTEE RULES. Ask one of your own state legislators or call the committee clerk to find out the requirements: Do witnesses have to sign up a half hour or more before the hearing begins? (Your own legislator's staff will usually be happy to sign you up to testify before the hearing starts so you don't have to arrive as early.) Also, how much time does each witness have to speak?

◆ USE YOUR TIME WISELY. Plot how to best use the two to five minutes that each witness or organization will be allotted. Be brief and be compelling. Use facts as well as personal stories. Write a statement that can be distributed to each member of the committee. Bring extra copies for reporters, other legislators who are not committee members, and the staff.

◆ DISTRIBUTE YOUR SPEECH. Decide who can take care of faxing your testimony to the Associated Press (AP), daily newspapers, and TV stations before the hearing, in the hopes of getting reporters to attend.

◆ DESIGN VISUALS. Graphs, posters, or a stack of pledge cards will liven up your testimony and help attract the attention of legislators and the news media. Committee members sit through hours and hours of long, boring speeches; your challenge is to keep them awake and interested.

◆ SPEAK RATHER THAN READ. Bring your written statement to hand out to the committee and the press, but don't read it. Good arguments and good eye contact will keep everyone's attention.

◆ BE SEEN. While you're at the statehouse, be sure to stop by the offices of your own state representatives and senators. Keep in mind how important their staff assistants are, too.

(Also refer to *Chapter 3: Face-Time and Presentation Pointers.*)

TESTIMONY TO LEGISLATORS

Here's an example of written testimony plus a hand-drawn state map that helped persuade a majority of Maryland representatives and senators to grant limited voting rights to the student member of the state board of education.

EMANUEL TSOUROUNIS, II, REPRESENTATIVE *Your name and affiliation*
MARYLAND ASSOCIATION OF STUDENT COUNCILS
VERBAL TESTIMONY/HOUSE OF DELEGATES WAYS AND MEANS
COMMITTEE—MARCH 4, 1993

RE: HOUSE BILL 585 ◀ **2** *Specific legislation*

Ladies and gentlemen of the committee, good afternoon. Today is quite an exciting day in the world of students. After eight years, we, the students, come one step closer to saying that our voice has been truly heard. I am, of course, speaking of House Bill 585, which, if **3** ▶ passed, would grant the student member of the Maryland State Board of Education a vote on most issues presented before the Board. I support this movement, as well as my constituents from *Speak from your head and heart* Calvert County and around the state. Further, I request your support of the bill and ask that you send it back to the floor of the House of Delegates with your unanimous support. ◀ **4** *Spell out what action you want them to consider!*

5 Student representation is nothing new to the State of Maryland. With the addition of Calvert County this year, nineteen out of twenty-five Maryland school boards, including the Maryland State Board of Education, have some form of student representation to their school *Provide facts* board. This number accounts for 76% of the total number of school boards in the state. Among these school boards, the Anne Arundel County student board member possesses full voting rights and the student of the Montgomery County Board of Education has limited voting rights.

6 These figures mean nothing, however, unless recognition is given for the number of requests made to grant new or extended voting rights to student board positions. This year, five such requests have been *Include* made. These requests, made for the positions of student member of *relevant* the Maryland State Board of Education, Baltimore County, *statistics* Montgomery County, and Prince George's County Boards of Education, and the Board of School Commissioners of Baltimore City, represent a change of status for the student members of five out of a possible nineteen school boards. Its meaning, simply put, is that the success of student members is incredible. Thus, logically, an increase in responsibility by means of a vote is in order.

YOUTH!

How would you feel, if you came to this building knowing that you must take a position on issues presented that are in the best interest of your constituency and knowing how incapable you are of confirming your positions. You have no vote, no voice. Of course, you can offer your opinions and yes, you do have an official title, but you have no validity to your position. That is the same situation as the Student Member of the Maryland State Board of Education is in. He or she comes to each board meeting and is allowed to debate issues and policies, but has no way to have his or her position accounted. It is frustrating to the member, but also for the hundreds of thousands of students who remain unheard because the voice of the student member is not recognized. The students are ready to accept the responsibility of the vote. Are we not deserving? It is necessary that the position of the student member include a vote. How would you feel if you were in our shoes? Thank you.

7

Engage your audience

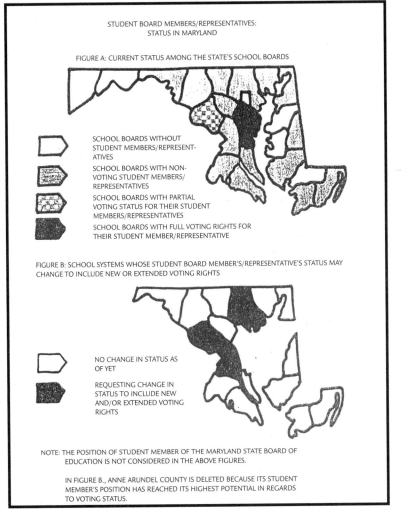

STUDENT BOARD MEMBERS/REPRESENTATIVES:
STATUS IN MARYLAND

FIGURE A: CURRENT STATUS AMONG THE STATE'S SCHOOL BOARDS

SCHOOL BOARDS WITHOUT STUDENT MEMBERS/REPRESENT-ATIVES

SCHOOL BOARDS WITH NON-VOTING STUDENT MEMBERS/REPRESENTATIVES

SCHOOL BOARDS WITH PARTIAL VOTING STATUS FOR THEIR STUDENT MEMBERS/REPRESENTATIVES

SCHOOL BOARDS WITH FULL VOTING RIGHTS FOR THEIR STUDENT MEMBER/REPRESENTATIVE

FIGURE B: SCHOOL SYSTEMS WHOSE STUDENT BOARD MEMBER'S/REPRESENTATIVE'S STATUS MAY CHANGE TO INCLUDE NEW OR EXTENDED VOTING RIGHTS

NO CHANGE IN STATUS AS OF YET

REQUESTING CHANGE IN STATUS TO INCLUDE NEW AND/OR EXTENDED VOTING RIGHTS

NOTE: THE POSITION OF STUDENT MEMBER OF THE MARYLAND STATE BOARD OF EDUCATION IS NOT CONSIDERED IN THE ABOVE FIGURES.

IN FIGURE B., ANNE ARUNDEL COUNTY IS DELETED BECAUSE ITS STUDENT MEMBER'S POSITION HAS REACHED ITS HIGHEST POTENTIAL IN REGARDS TO VOTING STATUS.

8

Use a map, graph or some other visual

CHAPTER 5
Keep Plugging Away

Like any adventure, your campaign is bound to have its ups and downs.

Remember change **takes time and rarely happens quickly.**

You might run up against a **powerful** well-funded **opposition.**

It may be very challenging!
You probably will need to respond to new situations, evaluate your progress and adjust your goals accordingly.

Don't give up - be persistent.

Learn from setbacks and defeat.

Celebrate victories both big and small.

A few strategies are spelled out in this final chapter to keep you and your teammates motivated during the last phase of your campaign, especially when faced with potential difficulties.

Flash back
Flash back
Flash back
Flash back
Flash back

EVALUATING YOUR PROGRESS

Flash back to when you first got the inkling to act. Do you remember those first thoughts you had? Your original goals? The plan you and your teammates developed? Glance at the notes you jotted down, especially those from when you were first searching for a solution or inventing an appropriate name for your group. What's happened so far? How have your goals or plan of action changed? Have you achieved what you set out to do?

Individually and as a group, evaluate your progress. Devote time at the end of every meeting to see how everybody feels and review the latest developments. If most of the team has online access, e-mail and chat rooms offer a faster way to talk things out. A lot is gained by analyzing every stage of your campaign. It can help you spot new opportunities and figure out your next move. Listening to one another's reactions also will unify the group. All the different ideas expressed serve as a reminder of the team's combined brainpower and energy.

As each event occurs, examine it on two levels. First, you might want to share **personal impressions** and **expectations.** Next, talk together about how well the team functions and your progress in realizing your goal. Let's say you just met with a key decision-maker who made flattering and supportive comments, but refused to make any commitment. Take a few minutes to dissect the exchange. Talk about how you were treated and how well all of you worked as a team. Discuss what you would do differently in a similar situation. Think about what information might have been more persuasive with the VIP. Then decide on an immediate follow-up action and explore possible next steps.

Sometimes your judgement of the situation and the feedback you get from others will cause you to modify your goals, revise your strategies, and experiment with new tactics. After all, situations change. Time schedules are altered. You might have hit a roadblock or your campaign has stalled. When you launched this project weeks or months ago, there was no way to predict what would actually happen. So as you evaluate this **evolving adventure** and reshape your game plan, pay attention to the same considerations you weighed when you first started, including:

TIMING—Comedians know t i m i n g i s c r u c i a l and the same holds true for activists. You may realize now that your proposal cannot be considered for a couple of months, until the school board meets or because the state legislature is not in session. Does it make sense to continue to build public support or would it be wiser to direct your energy to a different short-term goal? Another possibility is to put aside your top concern and **speak out** on related issues that are actively being debated and in the news.

FRAMING—It might make sense to change how you have been presenting or "framing" your plan. Sometimes it may be smarter to avoid controversy and remain low-key so as not to stir up the opposition. In other cases, the opposite may be true. A proposal may not get the attention it deserves because it doesn't seem new and different, so the challenge will be to **make your initiative stand out**. Constantly rethink your message and sound bite. When reconsidering how to present your plan, never misrepresent or distort.

MOBILIZING—Are there enough people on your side? Is it necessary to drum up more support? Are you targeting the right audience? Do you have a sponsor or champion for your cause who is **influential** enough with other decision-makers?

As you evaluate your progress, you may realize just how often you and your team are tested. Most likely you will have to **prove repeatedly** that this youth-led initiative is not merely for class credit or to enhance your résumé. Even those who seem not to question your motives may be patronizing. Perseverance means interpreting a brush-off or polite "no" as a challenge. Often it is the second or third time when your group returns to make their case to decision-makers that they begin to really listen and you get results.

DARE TO DREAM AND DON'T GIVE UP

Everyone is challenged, but the key is to not give up. Remember that most people who succeed fail at first. Look at the record of disappointments that occurred in this remarkable man's life:

AGE 22	FAILED in business.
AGE 23	DEFEATED as a candidate to the state legislature.
AGE 24	AGAIN FAILED in business.
AGE 25	Elected to state legislature.
AGE 26	GIRLFRIEND DIED.
AGE 27	SUFFERED A NERVOUS BREAKDOWN.
AGE 29	DEFEATED for Speaker of the state legislature.
AGE 34	DEFEATED for U.S. House of Representatives.
AGE 37	Elected to U.S. House of Representatives.
AGE 39	LOST his reelection.
AGE 46	DEFEATED for U.S. Senator.
AGE 47	DEFEATED for Vice President.
AGE 49	DEFEATED for U.S. Senator.
AGE 51	ELECTED PRESIDENT OF THE UNITED STATES.

The person who overcame one loss after another was Abraham Lincoln.

COMPETING IDEAS AND COMPROMISING

As you knew from the beginning of your initiative, not everyone is going to agree with you. **It's normal for people to disagree.** Some people will not understand what you are attempting to do or won't see the need for change. They may prefer the status quo to taking risks and trying new things. Others might reject your proposal because they favor other solutions or have a vested interest in keeping things the same. To them, your idea could seem threatening, especially if it will disrupt their way of living or reduce their power.

> **"In the middle of difficulty lies opportunity."**
> — Albert Einstein

Overcoming resistance will be a major challenge, especially if you are up against a well-organized and well-financed opposition. Up to this stage, you may have tried a number of tactics: writing letters, going to meetings, testifying before legislative committees, and applying public pressure. Still, decision-makers may not be supportive. It may be based on their strong ties to powerful established organizations. A decision-maker may believe the negative aspects of your initiative would outweigh the positive ones. For instance, your proposal to protect the environment might reduce waste, but drive up prices and increase taxes. Your elected official, on the other hand, may support low taxes and fewer business restrictions. The problem also may be so complex that agreeing on how to address it can be equally difficult.

If you find that your efforts are going nowhere, you might ask to sit down with the decision-makers to try to work out a deal. **Compromising is an inevitable part of the democratic process** and involves give-and-take until all sides arrive at a mutually acceptable solution. A compromise proposal does not necessarily mean that one side wins and the other loses. Rather, the search for the middle ground represents respect and tolerance for some very different opinions. Sometimes, the agreement that emerges may be better than the one you originally intended if it pieces together the best parts of several competing ideas and responds to different concerns. Compromising may also build greater unity in your community as well as commitment to seeking solutions to the problems you have identified.

YOUTH!

Anyone can be successful at compromising but it can be a stressful and lengthy task. People tend to feel very strongly about some issues and may have put lots of energy into fighting for their cause. You will need to be careful not to offend others, but also to protect yourself in the process. So here are some suggested strategies that can improve your chance for success.

Ten Commandments for Effective Compromise

REVIEW YOUR POSITION. As a team, discuss what is non-negotiable and what aspects of your proposal can be scaled back in order to move you closer to achieving your overall goal. Compromise requires give-and-take from both sides.

PATIENCE IS A VIRTUE. Don't compromise before you have to. Sometimes people give in or forfeit before they have heard what the other side will agree to. By doing so, they lose more than they win and shortchange their goals.

BE UP FRONT AND STATE YOUR EXPECTATIONS. Don't keep people guessing. Tell them exactly what you want, but keep it a secret what you might agree to.

LISTEN. It's the most important thing you can do.

BE UNDERSTANDING. Your attitude will be an important factor in how successful you are. Stay positive and open-minded and be respectful. Consider all your options.

BE ON GUARD. The motives of the people sitting across the table from you may be questionable. Protect yourself. Watch out for offers that sound good or reasonable, but water down your proposal too much. Don't make an agreement you know you should reject.

KEEP UP THE PRESSURE. Publicize your position and show evidence of community support through endorsements and favorable newspaper editorials. Continue to get supporters to write letters and telephone key decision-makers during negotiations.

IGNORE PERSONAL ATTACKS.

If you are treated rudely by others, don't counter-attack. You may, however, raise the issue of respect and question their intentions. Remember, argue over principles, not personalities.

AVOID OVERKILL. Being overly insistent can be counter-productive, especially if you are alienating others. If you don't seem to be making progress, step away from the table for a moment or move on to another related issue.

DEMONSTRATE YOUR COMMITMENT.

Your dedication will earn respect. The people you are negotiating with will be more willing to compromise if they know that you care and won't quit.

Watch Out for Weak Compromises

26% at work

Playing Up Endorsements and Support

In their testimony before the Maryland state legislature, five eighth grade girls pushing to ban spring-loaded, steel jaw traps strongly opposed a compromise amendment saying, "We are against elected officials getting credit in an election year for passing what looks like an animal rights bill, but really isn't." They successfully persuaded lawmakers to reject "this killer amendment," and a stronger bill passed which made these leg-hold traps illegal.

As part of a successful year-long campaign to get two students appointed to the Connecticut Board of Education, the International Student Activism Alliance continually publicized letters of support it received from state legislators and other influential people who endorsed student representation.

Remember that change is a gradual process. You may not get very far on your first attempt and may have to discuss some points over and over again. Make sure that everyone understands what you want to do and why. At the same time, try to understand their ideas and counter-proposals. In the end, you may not get everything you had hoped for, but you might make significant progress in the right direction. There will always be opportunities to try again in the future. Never stop trying!

YOUTH!

BE A MIRROR: REFLECT!

During the busiest phases of your campaign, probably the furthest thing from your mind will be to reflect about what is happening. You might be preparing to give a speech or thinking about how you can recover from an unexpected snafu that has disrupted your plan of action. The last thing you need is something else to do. Even so, give yourself some time along the way — not just at the end of a project or campaign — to sit back and think about what you are doing, what has been accomplished, and also what you are learning. Good memories and even bad ones begin to fade quickly and deserve to be remembered.

Reflecting can be a highly personal activity, or one that involves others. Some groups may want to sit around after a meeting to talk about what they've done while others might prefer individually to jot down notes in their journals, like "Download Your Brain," included at the end of this chapter. Others use a tape recorder or video camera to capture and record for posterity their accomplishments, as well as difficult moments when they didn't know how they'd pull through. You may also want to create a portfolio with copies of your speeches, press releases, letters, newspaper clips, and news broadcasts, too. **Please don't lose this history!** Try to . . .

Judge what impact you have made in terms of the problem you set out to work on.

Imagine how you might continue to be active in the future.

Think about all the ways you have grown and changed.

Summarize what you have learned and the knowledge you've gained.

Categorize the skills you've acquired, often through trial and error.

Remember your most loyal supporters and most unlikely allies.

Assess how adults treated you as well as those people you sought to influence.

Reflect on how the decision-making process could be more open to young people.

Consider how you can continue to inspire others to participate and try to make a difference, maybe even personally helping them to get involved.

Students thank forum attendees

The first ever Regional Education Forum consisting of students and school superintendents from the Greater Bridgeport region was conducted on March 12 in Bridgeport.

The forum was held by the Youth in Government Committee, a subcommittee of the RYASAP youth group in Bridge............ASAP youth gro.................ents fr.................

.....ull.

H.................
Sch.................gh
School for.................the forum.

Also, a thank you to the superintendents who attended, including Armand Fabri (Bridgeport Diocese school system), Norm Michaud (Monroe superintendent), Edwin T. Merritt (Trumbull superintendent), Dan Shamus (Bridgeport assistant superintendent) and Raymond O'Connell (Stratford superintendent). We especially thank O'Connell for attending since only one student from Stratford came to the forum.

Also, thanks to Pat Miller, head of Health/Physical Education curriculum in Fairfield public schools, for substituting for Fairfield Supt. Carol Harrington.

Unfortunately, the Easton/Redding regional superintendent did not attend and neither did any students from Joel Barlow High School of Easton/Redding.

Rachel Lowe
Fairfield High School
RYASAP Youth Committee chair-person

Naina Dhingra
Sara Mastrony
Fairfield High School
Youth in Government co-chairs

Capturing your thoughts now will be a great reminder of this experience in the future and can even help you in other endeavors. You never know when an event from your past will make an ideal topic for a class essay, in preparing college applications, or for job interviews.

While recounting your experiences, certain people may stand out as being particularly helpful. Your friends and supporters will have dedicated a lot of time and effort to making your goal a reality. Recognize them, right from the beginning. Send short **handwritten** notes, and think about expressing your thanks to important decision-makers as well as their staff assistants. Other options include giving a certificate of appreciation or a small gift, or perhaps nominating key allies for an award sponsored by a major organization. An article in the newspaper publicly thanking those individuals who have given serious attention to your cause will mean a lot to them.

"HEAR YE, HEAR YE"

In addition to recognizing someone or some event, consider seeking an official proclamation or resolution. Proclamations and resolutions are routinely issued to dedicate a day or place or to praise a particular individual or group. They can be sponsored and signed by a city council member, mayor, congressperson, or governor. Usually it will be necessary for your group to draft the exact wording of the document and then allow about a month for the staff person in charge to see that the proposed proclamation moves through the process. Be sure to explore with them the possibility of holding the proclamation signing ceremony in a public place and also inviting the news media for a photo-op in order to receive maximum publicity.

YOUTH!

In addition, you and your teammates are equally worthy of recognition, so don't be bashful. Awards and scholarships are sponsored by a number of local, state, and national organizations, many of which specifically **champion ordinary young people** who are doing extraordinary things. The President's Environmental Youth Awards, Points of Light Foundation, REACT Take Action Awards, The Giraffe Project, and Youth Hall of Fame International are such honors and you might be eligible to be nominated. Many adults who have worked closely with you will be delighted to write a letter of recommendation on your behalf.

And don't forget to CELEBRATE! Even small victories that seem trivial often lead to other opportunities. This snowball effect produces **m o m e n t u m** . Relish each of these accomplishments. A deli or pizzeria might be willing to donate food for a party for your team and your allies. People who feel appreciated will stay involved. Their enthusiasm will be contagious and attract others to join the cause. Besides, celebrating boosts team morale and can help to pick up the energy level to move on to the next phase of your campaign.

> "Each time a [person] stands up for an ideal, or acts to improve the lot of others, or strikes out against injustice, he sends forth a tiny ripple of hope, and crossing each other from a million different centers of energy and daring those ripples, builds a current which can sweep down the mightiest walls of oppression and resistance."
> - Robert F. Kennedy

We want to thank you for **caring** enough to act and **remind** you that even if you lose this time, you are better **prepared** for the next battle.
"**YOU**"th are the **26% solution!**

DOWNLOAD YOUR BRAIN . . .

These blank
pages are
intended for you
to jot down
thoughts and
ideas you feel
are important.
Brainstorm,
make notes,
keep a log of
contacts, list
phone numbers
and addresses,
whatever. You
may even wish
to use this
space to capture
your memories.
However you
choose to do it,
record history
in the making.
Good luck!

YOUTH!

THE 26% SOLUTION

INDEX

YOUTH!

ORDER FORM

Activism 2000 PROJECT

- ❑ One copy of *YOUTH! THE 26% SOLUTION* at $14.95 plus $4.00 shipping.

- ❑ The 17-minute video, "Influential Young Advocates" for $20.00 (shipping included).

- ❑ *YOUTH INFUSION: INTERGENERATIONAL ADVOCACY TOOLKIT,* **that contains the** *Guide,* **Influential Young Advocates video, and** *Youth! The 26% Solution* **handbook at $75 each (plus $6 s/h).**

- ❑ One copy of *NO KIDDING AROUND! AMERICA'S YOUNG ACTIVISTS ARE CHANGING OUR WORLD & YOU CAN TOO* by Wendy Schaetzel Lesko published in 1992 (260 pages) for $18.95 plus $4.00 shipping.

- ❑ Please add me to your mailing list so I can receive free mailings and notice of upcoming publications and special offers.

CALL 1-800-KID-POWER FOR MULTIPLE COPY DISCOUNTS!

The larger the quantity, the more you save.
YOUTH! THE 26% SOLUTION makes a great giveaway at conferences!

- ◆ Major discounts offered to youth-run groups
- ◆ Significant savings to non-profit and community organizations
- ◆ Bulk rates available to schools and government agencies
- ◆ Overnight delivery via UPS available

CALL 1-800-KID-POWER FOR PRICE/SHIPPING QUOTE.

100% MONEY BACK GUARANTEE

Please make check payable to the ACTIVISM 2000 PROJECT (Federal I.D. 521313350).

Total Purchase including shipping *(Maryland add 5% sales tax)* $ _____

❑ **Check or Money Order** - Amount Enclosed: $ _____
Credit Card ❑ VISA ❑ MasterCard ❑ Discover ❑ American Express

Credit Card #_____ Expiration Date _____

Signature_____

❑ **Purchase Order** PO # _____

NAME _____

ORGANIZATION_____

STREET ADDRESS _____

CITY/STATE _____ ZIP _____

TELEPHONE _____ E MAIL_____

Return to: ACTIVISM 2000 PROJECT, PO Box E, Kensington, MD 20895
info@youthactivism.com ◆ www.youthactivism.com
Toll-Free: 1-800-KID-POWER (1-800-543-7693) Fax: 301-929-8907